Seven

on the

Seventh ...

One Hundred

Dinners Honoring

CODY

Linda Barrasse and Friends

Seven on the Seventh … One Hundred Dinners Honoring Cody

iUniverse books may be ordered through booksellers or by contacting:

iUniverse
1663 Liberty Drive
Bloomington, IN 47403
www.iuniverse.com
844-349-9409

ISBN: 978-1-6632-1768-4 (sc)
ISBN: 978-1-6632-1766-0 (hc)
ISBN: 978-1-6632-1767-7 (e)

Library of Congress Control Number: 2021914473

Print information available on the last page.

iUniverse rev. date: 07/23/2021

Seven
on the
Seventh ...
One Hundred
Dinners Honoring
CODY

February 9, 1991- April 7, 2013

Cody Jude Barrasse died at twenty-two years old on April 7, 2013, after being hit by a car as a pedestrian. *Seven on the Seventh* describes the journey of his friends and family who were determined to keep his spirit alive.

For one hundred months, they have met for dinner at 7:00 p.m. on the seventh of each month to remember Cody. During these dinners, the seed for a very special foundation was planted. The seed grew into a tremendous organization run by Cody's brother, Joseph, along with Cody's friends who simply loved him.

Read on to understand how The Cody Barrasse Memorial Foundation transformed from a mere idea to a powerful force here to stay … All of this ignited with the fuel from *One Hundred Dinners Honoring Cody*.

This love story is dedicated to my two greatest accomplishments.

Their names are Joseph and Cody Barrasse.

→

Acknowledgements

Cover: Patrick Mineo and Michael Belardi

Artwork and doodles: Maryellen D'Andrea

Editing: Olivia D'Andrea

Strategy, Information Technology, and Best All-Around Teammate: Joseph Barrasse

x

Contents

Instructions: How to Use and Understand This Book

You are about to see dozens of recipes.

Some are my very own, usually made out of desperation with items I had in my cabinets.

Some were handed down to me from my Mom, Aunts, and other magnificent senior cooks.

Some were from friends who joined us for dinner to add to what I had already prepared.

And many were inspired by recipes found in cookbooks, magazines, and websites.

I have tweaked all of them to my liking, and I suggest you do the same. Add or subtract. Make it firmer or softer; more fudgy or more cake-like. Make it spicier or sweeter. It's *your* choice. These are now *your* recipes too.

The purpose of this book is not to promote that I am a brilliant creator of recipes … because I am not. It is to tell the story of my sons, Cody's Foundation, and how the whole thing started and revolved around food—great food that has been inspired by great recipes from multiple sources.

I learned to cook from an Italian Mom and loving, *Everybody Loves Raymond*–type Aunts. There was always lots of noise, flour all over the place, and a real sense of being loved.

Measuring was not their strong point; nor is it mine.

For some of these recipes, I have made educated guesses on the quantities suggested.

Yes, a handful of grated Parmesan cheese is not the same for all hands. As I instructed my son Joseph when he made his first lasagna, "OK, your hand is bigger than mine, so use three handfuls instead of four. Don't make a major production out of it!"

Experiment. Try it out. But mostly, have fun …

And enjoy every morsel.

Here's one last piece of instructional material before you start …

At the beginning of each chapter, you will learn about Cody and what has transpired throughout these past one hundred months. To understand the entire story as it happened, you can read the beginnings of each chapter through the "Epilogue." Then you can browse through all of the foods we have shared.

You also need to know the players:

I am Linda, Cody's mom.

Michael is Cody's dad.

Joseph is Cody's brother, older by three years.

The kids are all of Cody's and Joseph's friends who, from day one, were determined to honor their beloved friend and who continue to come for dinner each month at *Seven on the Seventh*.

Introduction

On April 7, 2013, I saw my darkest day. Our son, brother, and friend, Cody Jude Barrasse, died after being hit by a car as a pedestrian. He was twenty-two years old and was visiting friends at the University of Pittsburgh, just a few weeks shy of his graduation from Penn State University as a finance major.

It was supposed to be fun, but not this time. Cody sustained a brain injury that he could never survive.

Cody was the toughest person I knew. He was the most courageous, and he was the most true to himself of *anyone* I have ever met. As his final act of courage, he gave the ultimate gift—*himself*.

He donated all of his solid organs and multiple tissues to many people. Cody lives on.

On May 7, 2013, just one month after his death, we had our first dinner. I made a pot of vodka sauce—one of Cody's favorites—and invited all of his friends to join. More than fifty showed up. It was very important to me that his friends felt comfortable returning to the home they enjoyed … never to be afraid or reluctant.

Since that first and simple dinner in 2013, we have shared a meal for one hundred months. The kids come at 7:00 p.m. on the seventh of each month. Cody's friends continue to come, and I will continue to cook—until I take my last breath.

There is no better way to honor my son. He simply loved when his friends were in our home … and eating.

Sometimes the crowd is large; sometimes it's small. Doesn't matter. I will cook if only one can come.

During that first dinner in May 2013, several of my friends just showed up. They came to serve, they came to clean up, and they came because they loved me … as they loved Cody.

Since then, the so-called senior group continues to join in our monthly dinners. Not everyone is there every month, but they are all there at some point. They bring food ranging from appetizers to desserts to add to whatever I might be preparing. They clean, they grill, and they serve. But most importantly, they honor Cody.

I always wanted to write a book. Now, I have what, at first glance, appears to be a cookbook. I call it a non-cookbook. Yes, there are recipes, all of which I have made over the past one hundred months. Also included are many of the recipes made by this magnificent group of friends who continue to show up.

But what this book really is, is a love story …

It's a story of how twenty-two-year-old kids, with the guidance of Cody's twenty-five-year-old brother, put their loving energy into the great work of forming the Cody Barrasse Memorial Foundation.

This book will tell you about Cody, who he was, and what he did.

It will guide you down the journey of his foundation.

And it will teach you that even terrible life tragedies can be transformed into powerfully positive energy.

In this case, it all started (and usually ends) around food.

Now, read through these pages …

Make some of the recipes …

Enjoy the food …

And smile when you think of Cody!

Linda and Friends

Each month, dinner starts with a prayer.

Chapter 1:

Start-Ups

Why appetizers? Why don't we just dive right into that big, fat steak?

Eating appetizers is the time to get to know one another, to chat, to ask questions, to warm up to those around us, and to explore our dreams. Appetizers get us excited about what else is yet to come.

In our case, it all started around a pesto pizza and a board of cheeses intertwined with prosciutto, Soppressata, and lonza—all cured Italian meats.

Cody loved to nosh; appetizers were some of his favorites. It was his warm-up to the rest of his meal, which he always made an adventure.

During that first dinner on May 7, the concept of a memorial event was conceived. We were all hurting. We still could not wrap our heads around the brutal fact that Cody was gone. The kids simply would not accept the possibility that Cody could be forgotten … neither could I. That was really my greatest fear.

A few of the boys had the fledgling idea of having a three-on-three basketball tournament in Cody's memory. It would be open to everyone: athletes and those less competitive, young and old, short and tall.

My heart smiled at the thought. Not much brought greater joy to Cody's soul than to play a pick-up game of three-on-three.

He played by few rules: lots of contact, few fouls called, and, I am sure, many incidents that I never knew about. (Sometimes, it is really best that mothers don't know everything.)

The only real rule was that even the least of us would be welcome. That's just who Cody was. He had a way of lifting the lowest to the highest.

And so, the seed was planted …

The kids wanted the tournament to be in August, the month just before everyone went on to their respective grad schools or their new jobs.

They also wanted it to be at Scranton Prep, the Jesuit school that taught Cody more than reading, writing, and arithmetic. It preached the virtues of St. Ignatius … primarily of the importance of being "men and women for others."

Although Cody was born with the greatest sense of social justice, the Jesuits' mission was accomplished through Cody … *and* with all of these special young men and women, known as the kids. Cody was always the advocate for the underdog. He went out of his way to help those no one else would help. He led by his example, and his friends picked up from where he left off.

Now, they just needed to water that precious seed, warm it with the sun's rays, and nurture it into the event they wanted. But how could they do this in such a short period of time?

Off they went with their unstoppable energy. Joseph, Michael, and I were still numb, but these kids gave us energy and courage when we didn't have it on our own.

In just a few short weeks, we held our first basketball tournament. On August 10, 2013, fifty teams played to honor my son. They played in Scranton Prep's gym on the same floor where Cody made layups, boxed out his opponents, and cheered on his teammates.

And so, the story begins …
The seed will now have roots.

1. Asian Beef Skewers

Inspired by Allrecipes.

This is a simple do-ahead appetizer that is a great way to kick off a summer dinner.

Ingredients

1 1/2 pounds flank steak
2 green onions, chopped
1/4 cup low-sodium soy sauce
3 tablespoons hoisin sauce
3 tablespoons sherry
1 tablespoon minced fresh ginger
3 cloves garlic, minced
1 teaspoon barbeque sauce
16 (8-inch) skewers, soaked in water 30 minutes if wood or bamboo

Freeze flank steak 30 minutes to firm up and make it easier to slice.

Meanwhile, stir together green onions, soy sauce, hoisin, sherry, ginger, garlic, and barbeque sauce in a small bowl.

Cut flank steak across the grain into about 48 pieces (1/4-inch thick). Transfer to a 1-gallon ziplock plastic bag and pour sauce over steak. Massage bag to mix well and then chill for 2 hours.

Preheat an outdoor grill to high heat (450–650 degrees F). Remove steak from the bag, discarding marinade, and thread three slices on to each skewer. (Skewers can be assembled 8 hours ahead of time and chilled, covered, and then grilled right before serving.)

Lightly oil grill grate. Grill skewers 1 minute per slice for medium rare or to desired doneness.

2. Baked Crab Cakes

Inspired by Rita from FOOD.

Crab Cakes are historically fried. When serving a large crowd, this can often be a difficult task. These baked cakes are great for a crowd.

Prep time: 15 minutes
Total time: 30 minutes
Serves: 4–6

Ingredients

1 egg
3 tablespoons mayonnaise (I use horseradish sauce instead of mayo.)
1 tablespoon Worcestershire sauce
1 tablespoon Dijon mustard
2 teaspoons fresh lemon juice
1 tablespoon parsley, minced
1 scallion, finely chopped
1/2 cup bread crumbs
1/4 cup grated cheese
1 teaspoon Old Bay Seasoning
1 red bell pepper, chopped
1 pound lump crabmeat
1 tablespoon olive oil
tartar or cocktail sauce

Directions

Preheat oven to 375 degrees F.

Mix all cake ingredients together except for crabmeat and oil.

Gently toss in crabmeat and form eight patties. (If used as an appetizer, you can make sixteen small patties.)

Place on a sprayed sheet pan and sprinkle each lightly with olive oil.

Bake for 15 minutes.

Serve with favorite tartar sauce or cocktail sauce.

3. Fig Jam and Brie Tartlets

Inspired by my cousin Suzanne's wedding. When I tasted them, they were heavenly, and I thought, *I can make these!*

Ingredients

1 jar fig jam
1 wheel of Brie
frozen phyllo tartlets, thawed

Directions

Preheat oven to 350 degrees F.

Cut brie into small pieces that can fit into each tartlet.

Spread jam on top of brie.

Bake for about 10 minutes or until heated through and cheese is soft.

Most often, there are a dozen tartlets per box. If you can find tartlets that are not frozen, these can be used as a good substitute.

4. Balsamic Fig and Caramelized Onion Spread

Inspired by *Pesto, Tapenades, and Spreads* by Stacey Printz, 2009.

This is a great appetizer for any season. It's quick and easy to make and makes those with a discriminate palate smile.

Makes 1 1/2 cups.

Ingredients

1 tablespoon plus 1/3 cup olive oil
1 medium red onion, chopped
1 cup chopped Black Mission figs
1/4 cup plus 2 tablespoons balsamic vinegar
salt and freshly ground pepper
3–4 teaspoons honey

Directions

Heat 1 tablespoon of oil over medium heat.

Sauté the onion until soft and beginning to brown, about 4 minutes.

Add figs and 1/4 cup balsamic vinegar and continue to sauté until most of the liquid is gone and the mixture is slightly caramelized, 2–3 minutes.

Transfer the fig mixture to the food processor. Add the remaining 2 tablespoons vinegar and season with salt and pepper. Add honey.

Pulse until the ingredients start to come together.

With the machine running, gradually stream in the remaining 1/3 cup oil and pulse until a coarse paste forms.

Serve with your favorite crackers or crostini along with goat cheese.

5. Caponata

Inspired by Joanne Santarelli.

This recipe is filled with very Sicilian ingredients. I had this many years ago at a Christmas party. I simply loved it, and the woman who made it was kind enough to send me her recipe. It's been one of my favorite appetizers since and can be made several days in advance.

Makes about 4 cups

Ingredients

2 medium eggplants, peeled and cut into cubes
kosher salt
1 1/2 cups olive oil
1 medium onion, diced
6 celery ribs cut into small pieces
1 cup pitted green olives, chopped
3/4 cup capers
1 1/2 cups tomato sauce (recipe to follow)
1/2 cup red wine vinegar or balsamic vinegar
2 tablespoons sugar

Directions

Sprinkle kosher salt over eggplant cubes and allow to drain on a paper towel for 1 hour.

Rinse and dry.

Fry in 1 cup oil until golden. Drain on a paper towel.

In the same pan, sauté onion and celery in 1/2 cup oil.

Then add the olives, capers, sauce, vinegar, and sugar. Simmer for 5–10 minutes.

Stir in eggplant and simmer an additional 0 minutes.

Taste to see if salt needs to be added.

Refrigerate for 24 hours. Serve with crusty bread, crostini, or your favorite crackers.

6. Chicken Satay with Peanut Sauce

Inspired by Food Network.

This recipe combines an interesting combination of Eastern flavors, including everyone's favorite: peanut butter!

Total time: 2 hours, 40 minutes (includes marinating time)
Makes 20 skewers.

Ingredients

Chicken
2 pounds chicken tenders
1 cup plain yogurt
1 tablespoon curry powder
4 dashes hot sauce (or to taste)
3 cloves garlic, minced
1 shallot, minced
1-inch piece ginger, minced
kosher salt

Peanut Sauce
1 tablespoon vegetable oil
1 tablespoon curry powder
3 cloves garlic, minced
1 shallot, minced
1-inch piece ginger, minced
1/2 cup smooth peanut butter
1/2 cup coconut milk
1/4 cup soy sauce
2 tablespoons brown sugar
1/2 teaspoon hot chili oil
2 limes, juiced
kosher salt
1/2 cup hot water
1/2 cup chopped fresh cilantro for garnish

For the Chicken
Cut the tenders into 2-inch pieces and put in a large container.

Whisk together yogurt, curry powder, hot sauce, garlic, shallot, ginger, and some salt in a small bowl.

Pour over the chicken, cover, and marinate in the refrigerator for 1–2 hours.

In the meantime, soak the wooden skewers.

When ready to cook the chicken, heat grill pan or outdoor grill.

Remove chicken from the marinade and thread two pieces onto each skewer.

Grill the chicken until cooked through with nice grill marks, 3–4 minutes per side. Let cool, cover, and refrigerate

For the Peanut Sauce
Heat oil in a small pot.

Cook curry powder, garlic, shallot, and ginger until the aromatics are soft.

Scrape this into a blender and add coconut milk, peanut butter, soy sauce, brown sugar, hot chili oil, lime juice, and a pinch of salt. Blend, adding the hot water a little at a time to thin it out and make it smooth.

Transfer to a bowl, cover, and refrigerate.

To serve, put a small bowl or ramekin of peanut sauce in the middle of a round serving platter. Arrange the skewers on the platter around the peanut sauce. Sprinkle with cilantro.

7. Chickpea Salad with Lemon, Parmesan, and Fresh Herbs

Inspired by Bon Appétit.

This simple appetizer is light and fresh … and also healthy!

Prep time: 10 minutes
Serves: 8

Ingredients

1 (15-ounce) can chickpeas, rinsed and drained
3 tablespoons chopped fresh basil
2 tablespoons chopped fresh Italian parsley
2 tablespoons fresh lemon juice
4 teaspoons extra-virgin olive oil
1 clove garlic, minced
1/3 cup grated Parmesan cheese
kosher salt

Directions

Combine chickpeas, basil, parsley, lemon juice, extra-virgin olive oil, and minced garlic in a medium bowl.

Add grated Parmesan and toss gently to blend all ingredients. Season with salt and pepper to taste.

Can be made 4 hours ahead. Cover and refrigerate. Serve chilled or at room temperature.

8. Guacamole by Cindy

This different twist on guacamole was given to me by my incredible roommate, Cindy West. I treasure it, as I treasure her friendship over the last forty-four years.

Ingredients

3–4 avocados
kosher salt
1/4 teaspoon cayenne pepper (or to taste)
2 limes, juiced
3–4 sprigs of basil, cut into thin strips

Directions

Mash all ingredients together.

Serve with your favorite chips.

9. Clams Casino

by Laurie Quinn

Laurie Quinn is mother to one of Cody's closet friends, Christopher. She has been coming to our dinners faithfully and has added many of her own dishes to our meals. Here is one of her biggest hits.

Ingredients

4 cans minced clams, drain 2 and save the liquid from the other 2
1 stack plus 6 round butter crackers, crumbled
11 slices bacon, fried and crumbled
1 medium onion, minced
3 stalks celery, minced
1 medium green pepper, minced
1 stick butter

Directions

Preheat oven to 350 degrees F.

Sauté vegetables in 1 stick butter.

Mix well with all other ingredients.

Bake for about 20 minutes.

10. Curried Chickpeas

Inspired by Rachel Ray.
Total time: 10 minutes
Serves: 8

Ingredients

1 large onion, chopped
3 cloves garlic, minced
2 tablespoons extra-virgin olive oil
2 (15-ounce) cans chickpeas, drained and rinsed
1 (6-ounce) package spinach
3 tablespoons tomato paste
2 teaspoons curry powder
plain yogurt for topping

Directions

In a large skillet, cook onion and garlic in extra-virgin olive oil over medium heat for 5 minutes.

Add next four ingredients and 1/3 cup water.

Cook 2 minutes

Season with salt and pepper to taste.

Top with yogurt.

Serve with your favorite cracker or bread.

11. Grilled Bratwurst in Beer

Inspired by FOOD.

This is a great appetizer for a fun Oktoberfest dinner and brings a lot of smiles every time.

Total time: 55 minutes
Serves: 15 as an appetizer

Ingredients

10 bratwursts
2 (12-ounce) cans beer
2 large onions, chopped

Directions

Put two beers in a pot.

Throw in the onion and brats. If you need more water to cover brats, add water.

Bring the beer to a simmer. Do not let it boil. Boiling will cause brats to burst. When steam begins to rise from the top of the liquid, it is just right.

Simmer the brats for 20 minutes.

Remove the brats from the liquid and throw out the beer-and-onion mixture.

Grill brats and brown on all sides, about 10 minutes total.

Cut each brat into two pieces.

Dip in a good spicy mustard.

12. Hoagie Dip

This is another great appetizer from Laurie Quinn and tastes just like a hoagie!

Prep time: 30 minutes

pepperoni
salami
ham
provolone cheese
white and sharp cheddar cheese
red pepper
red onion
black olives
zesty Italian dressing
good crusty bread

Directions

Place all ingredients except for the dressing and bread into a large ziplock bag.

Add zesty Italian dressing to taste, but do not soak.

Allow to marinate in the refrigerator for several hours.

Transfer dip to a bowl and serve with slices of crusty bread.

13. Hot Reuben Dip in a Pumpernickel Bowl

Inspired by Food Network.

Total time: 50 minutes
Serves: 10

This is a great Super Bowl party appetizer! And there's no clean up … You eat the whole thing!

Ingredients

1/2 cup mayonnaise
3 tablespoons ketchup
3 tablespoons finely diced dill pickle
kosher salt and finely ground pepper
3 cups grated Swiss cheese (about 9 ounces)
2/3 cup sauerkraut, drained, rinsed, and roughly chopped

4 ounces cream cheese, room temperature
4 ounces chopped sliced pastrami
1 round or oval pumpernickel bread
extra-virgin olive oil for drizzling
crackers or crudités for serving

Directions

Preheat oven to 375 degrees F.

Wisk the mayonnaise, ketchup, and pickle in a large bowl until combined. Season with salt and pepper.

Add the Swiss cheese, sauerkraut, cream cheese, and pastrami to the mayonnaise mixture.

Stir with a rubber spatula until combined.

With a serrated knife, hollow out the loaf, leaving a 1/2-inch thick shell. Reserve cut-out bread and break into pieces.

Fill the loaf with dip and transfer to a baking sheet.

Bake the bread bowl until the cheese melts and the top is golden brown, about 30 minutes.

Drizzle the bread pieces with oil and salt. Add bread to the oven during the last 10 minutes of baking. Serve bread and dip warm.

14. Peach and Brie Quesadillas with Lime Honey Dipping Sauce

Inspired by MyRecipes.

Total time: 25 minutes
Serves: 4–6

This is an interesting twist on the classic quesadilla. Peaches and brie are a beautiful combination. Give it a try!

Ingredients

Sauce
3 tablespoons Honey
2 teaspoons fresh lime juice
1/2 teaspoon grated lime rind

Quesadillas
1 cup thinly sliced firm ripe peaches (I have also used frozen peaches.)
1 tablespoon chopped fresh chives
1 teaspoon brown sugar
4 ounces brie cheese, thinly sliced
4 (8-inch) flour tortillas
cooking spray

Directions

To prepare sauce, combine first three ingredients with whisk and set aside.

To prepare quesadillas, combine peaches, 1 tablespoon chives, and sugar, tossing gently to coat.

Heat a large nonstick skillet over medium-high heat.

Arrange one fourth of peach mixture and one fourth of cheese over half of each tortilla. Fold tortillas in half.

Coat pan with cooking spray. Place two quesadillas in pan; cook 2 minutes on each side, or until they are lightly browned and crisp.

Remove from pan and keep warm. Repeat with remaining quesadillas.

Cut each quesadilla into three wedges. Serve with sauce and garnish with chives.

15. Peppery Pesto Baked Wings

Inspired by *Rachel Ray Every Day*.

Wings are one of the biggest hits at our dinners. They are inhaled the second they are ready. This recipe is great for a crowd, as they are baked—a different version of a beloved appetizer.

Serves: 8

Ingredients

Wings
4 pounds chicken wings
2 tablespoons canola oil
1 tablespoon salt
2 teaspoons pepper, divided

Glaze
1 cup refrigerated pesto, divided
1/2 cup grated Parmesan cheese

Topping
crushed red pepper to taste

Directions

Position rack in the top third of the oven. Preheat to 450 degrees F. Line a large, rimmed baking sheet with foil. Set a wire rack inside the baking sheet and coat with cooking spray.

Cut off and discard wing tips from the chicken wings. Separate the flats from the drumettes and pat dry. In a large bowl, toss the wings with canola oil, salt, and 1 teaspoon of the pepper. Arrange on rack in a single layer. Bake until the skin is crispy, about 45 minutes.

Set 1/4 cup of the pesto aside and put the rest in a large bowl. Toss the wings in the pesto and then arrange them on the rack in a single layer.

Sprinkle with 1/4 cup of the Parmesan.

Bake until the glaze is shiny and browned in spots and the chicken is cooked through, about 10 minutes. Season with the remaining teaspoon of pepper.

Transfer wings to a platter. Dab with reserved pesto and sprinkle with crushed red pepper to taste.

16. Roasted Shrimp with Rosemary and Thyme

Inspired by *Fine Cooking*.

Total time: 30 minutes
Serves: 4

Ingredients

6 tablespoons extra-virgin olive oil
8 fresh thyme sprigs
6 large fresh rosemary sprigs, halved
1 teaspoon freshly ground pepper

1 1/2 pounds extra-large shrimp (26–30 per pound), peeled and deveined
1 1/2 tablespoons white wine vinegar
1/2 teaspoon kosher salt

Directions

Position rack in center of oven and heat to 400 degrees F.

Pour oil in 9- x 13-inch baking dish. Add thyme, rosemary, and pepper and bake until the oil mixture is fragrant, about 12 minutes.

Add the shrimp to the dish and toss with tongs until coated. Bake the shrimp until pink and firm, 8–19 minutes.

Add the vinegar and salt, toss well, and let rest at room temperature until the oil cools slightly, about 5 minutes. Serve.

17. Sausage Quiche Squares

Inspired by Laurie Quinn.

Prep time: 15 minutes
Cook time: 20 minutes
Makes 8 dozen

Ingredients

1 pound bulk Italian sausage
1 cup shredded cheddar cheese
1 cup shredded Monterey Jack cheese
1/2 cup finely chopped onion
1/2 can (2 ounces total) chopped chilis
1 tablespoon minced jalapeño pepper
10 large eggs
1 teaspoon chili powder
1 teaspoon ground cumin
1 teaspoon salt
1/2 teaspoon garlic powder
1/2 teaspoon pepper

Directions

Preheat oven to 375 degrees F.

In a large skillet, brown sausage and drain. Place in greased 9 x 13 baking dish.

Layer with cheeses, onion, chilis, and jalapeño.

In a bowl, beat eggs and spices and then pour over sausage mixture.

Bake until knife in center comes out clean, 18–23 minutes.

Cool 10 minutes. Cut into squares and enjoy!

18. Spinach and Mushroom Quesadillas

This is a great do-ahead appetizer. The quesadillas can be assembled several hours ahead and refrigerated until ready to bake.

Inspired by Martha Stewart.

Ingredients

2 tablespoons canola oil
2 medium red onions, thinly sliced
8 ounces button or cremini mushrooms, thinly sliced (I have also used shitake.)
12 ounces fresh spinach, shredded
coarse salt and ground pepper
8 flour tortillas
8 ounces pepper jack cheese, shredded

Directions

Preheat oven to 400 degrees F.

In a 12-inch skillet, warm 1 tablespoon oil over medium heat.

Cook onions until golden, about 5 minutes.

Add mushrooms, stirring occasionally until tender, about 6–8 minutes.

Add spinach in 2 batches, letting the first batch wilt slightly before adding the next. Cook until spinach is completely wilted and mixture is dry, 2–3 minutes total. Season with salt and pepper.

Brush one side of tortillas with remaining oil. Place four tortillas, oiled side down onto baking sheets.

Layer each tortilla with cheese, spinach mixture, and more cheese, dividing evenly.

Top with remaining 4 tortillas, oiled sides up, and lightly press to seal.

Bake until cheese has melted and tortillas are golden brown, turning them once, about 10 minutes.

Cut quesadillas into quarters and serve.

19. Summer Herbed Grilled Shrimp

Inspired by MyRecipes.

I love summer. I love herbs. I love shrimp … So perfect!

Prep time: 22 minutes
Total time: 30 minutes
Serves: 8 (serving size, 3 shrimp)

Ingredients

1/3 cup finely chopped flat-leaf parsley
1/4 cup finely chopped red onion
2 tablespoons grated lemon rind
1 tablespoon finely chopped fresh oregano
1 teaspoon minced garlic
1 1/2 pounds large shrimp, peeled and deveined
2 1/2 tablespoons extra-virgin olive oil, divided
1 tablespoon honey
1/2 teaspoon pepper
1/4 teaspoon kosher salt
cooking spray
1 1/2 teaspoons red wine vinegar

Directions

Preheat grill to medium-high heat.

Combine first five ingredients in a small bowl.

Combine shrimp, 1 tablespoon oil, honey, pepper, and salt in a large bowl. Toss gently to coat.

Arrange shrimp on grill rack coated with cooking spray. Grill 3 minutes on each side or until done. Remove shrimp from grill.

Stir remaining 1 1/2 tablespoons oil and vinegar into herb mixture. Top shrimp with herb mixture and toss all together.

20. Tater Tot Nachos

This is a variation of what we know as nachos. Whoever thought of it was a genius! But be warned …
You need a fork for these nachos. It's worth all the mess.

Ingredients

2-pound bag tater tots
1 pound ground beef, cooked and seasoned with taco seasoning
2 cups shredded cheese (can use a combination of Monterey Jack and cheddar)
salsa
guacamole (store-bought or homemade)
sour cream
olives
jalapeños

Directions

Preheat oven to 400 degrees F.

Place tater tots in 9- x 13-inch pan.

Spread meat over the top of potatoes.

Sprinkle cheese on top of meat.

Bake at for 35–40 minutes or until heated through.

Top with salsa.

Serve with guacamole, sour cream, olives, and jalapeños on the side.

21. Zucchini Garlic Bites

Inspired by Grow a Good Life.

This recipe was given to me by my faithful medical assistant, Sherrie. It's an addicting appetizer! You will make it over and over again.

Prep time: 12 minutes
Total time: 30 minutes
Makes 16 bites

Ingredients

1 cup shredded zucchini
1 egg
1/3 cup bread crumbs
1/4 cup grated Parmesan cheese
2 cloves finely grated garlic
2 tablespoons fresh chives chopped
1 tablespoon fresh parsley chopped
1 teaspoon fresh basil chopped
1 teaspoon fresh oregano chopped
pinch of salt and pepper
tomato sauce for dipping (The recipe for my marinara sauce can be found in chapter 4.)

Directions

Preheat oven to 400 degrees F. Lightly coat a baking sheet with olive oil or nonstick spray. Set aside.

Squeeze out any excess water from the zucchini.

In a medium bowl, add all the ingredients and mix well.

Shape a tablespoon of the mixture into your hands, pat into a small ball, and place on baking sheet. Repeat process with the remainder of the mixture.

Bake 15–18 minutes until golden. Serve warm with marinara sauce.

22. Smoked Salmon

Inspired by my cousins Joey and Jill Barrasse.

Someone once asked me, "Why do you go through all the trouble to smoke your own salmon when you can buy it?" The answer is simple: because it tastes so good.

My cousins Joey and Jill have perfected the art of smoking a salmon—truly a family favorite.

Total time: 3 hours
Serves: 10 as an appetizer

Ingredients

1 whole salmon fillet
extra-virgin olive oil
kosher salt
pepper
fresh dill

Directions

Lightly rub fillet with good olive oil.

Sprinkle with kosher salt and freshly ground pepper.

Sprinkle with fresh dill.

Place in smoker at 225 degrees F for 3 hours.

Serve at room temperature with cream cheese, capers, and red onion.

23. Pesto Pizza

Inspired by me. I just wanted a different kind of pizza to serve as an appetizer. This is simple and is always devoured.

Total time: 30 minutes
Serves: 10 as an appetizer (cut into party-size pieces)

Ingredients

1 store-bought pizza crust (homemade dough can always be used)
extra-virgin olive oil
bottled or homemade pesto
ripe tomatoes sliced about 1/4-inch thick
grated Parmesan cheese
shredded mozzarella cheese

Directions

Preheat oven to 350 degrees F.

Lightly coat both sides of pizza crust with extra-virgin olive oil.

Spread a thin layer of pesto sauce over the crust.

Top with tomato slices and sprinkle with Parmesan and mozzarella.

Bake for 20 minutes or until edges brown.

Cut into party-size pieces to serve.

24. Pulled Pork Nachos

Inspired by Joseph's college friend Danny. He told me about this concept over a great lunch one spring day in Boston. So, I gave it a try, and I may like them even more than traditional nachos!

Simply make Pulled Pork as described in chapter 5 of this book.

Then make the rest as you make traditional nachos

Possible garnishes:
avocado
salsa
sour cream
jalapeños, sliced
melted cheese (You can use queso, any bottled nacho cheese, or Velveeta.)
nacho chips of your choice

Place chips on a plate and top with heated pulled pork and all other ingredients of your choice.

There's no way around this: It is messy but worth every bit of it.

25. Rosie's Favorite Gauc by Sheila

Inspired by Sheila, chief grillmaster, guac maker, and bossy friend.

When Sheila would make this guacamole, our dear friend Rosie's mouth would water. Rosie, like Cody, was taken from us much too soon. So, Rosie, this one's for you.

Ingredients

6 ripe avocados
1 small onion, finely chopped
2 small Roma (or other) tomatoes, finely chopped
pinch of cayenne pepper
large pinch of garlic powder
1 tablespoon finely chopped cilantro
lemon or lime juice (I prefer lime.)

Directions

Mix the avocado, onion, tomato, and cilantro.

Add cayenne and garlic powder.

Don't be shy when mixing. You want the consistency to be such that you can scoop it with a chip.

Add a big squeeze of lemon or lime juice to coat and mix.

Enjoy with tortilla chips.

Chapter 2:

Soup's On

Soup is a food that warms our bodies and comforts our souls. That's why I make a pot every month for our dinners.

I wasn't so sure on that warm and beautiful day on August 10, 2013, that I would be terribly comforted.

I woke early. Registration for the first tournament was to start at eight o'clock that morning. I arrived at Scranton Prep at six thirty to display throughout Prep's lobby the many pictures of Cody I had collected. I wanted the participants to get a glimpse of the young man they were honoring.

I wore all of Cody's clothes that day (as I do every year) … a worn and very old cut-off shirt, his North Carolina Basketball shorts, and his size 12 high-top North Carolina powder-blue sneakers.

I cried all the way to Scranton Prep. Never had I gone to a basketball tournament unless I was going to watch Cody play, *not* to memorialize him.

Something was just not right …

I dried my eyes, picked up the shorts that were much too big for me, put my game face on, and then entered the school.

So many people gave of themselves to help this initial adventure happen. One of the devoted moms volunteered to be in charge of a basket raffle. She and one of my high school classmates lovingly collected many baskets to donate, and they set up a display that was spectacular. They received baskets from everywhere and effortlessly orchestrated the entire project.

The lobby was all set up. Cody's pictures were intertwined among raffle baskets, registration materials, and organ donation literature.

By this time, the teams were starting to register.

The place was manned completely by eager volunteers, most of whom had never done something like this before. The team brackets were masterminded by a few of Cody's friends. They worked right up to the last hours ensuring all players got their appointed games. Another booth showcased T-shirts with Cody's name and number 8 on the back, shorts with our logo, and more. Volunteers came out of the woodwork with the single purpose of making this event work. And it was all organized by the kids with Joseph's leadership.

Many of Cody's teachers were there. Some were scorekeepers, some sold raffle tickets, and some were just simply there. The Jesuits who nurtured him in his studies were filled with pride. Friends just showed up. Some ran a refreshment stand and even donated all the refreshments! Others were ready to take photos.

And then it was finally time for me to enter the gym. It took everything I had to open that door.

As I saw hundreds of kids wearing Cody's name on their backs playing for him, I cried once again. This time they were happy tears. The struggle finally stopped.

The room was filled with an overwhelming sense of positive energy. Cody *was* in that gym, and there was not a doubt about it. I saw only smiling faces wherever I turned.

In a short time, it would be *our* team's first round. (Yes, a few of the kids included me on their team.) I approached the foul line to take the shot that would determine who would have possession first.

Swoosh! The ball went right in—all net. A miracle had just happened. Cody surely guided that ball into the basket.

I managed to score six points that day—a total that was more than I had ever scored in my life.

The day was hectic, yet so gratifying. I was so proud of the kids. In the end, despite really missing their friend, they felt a great sense of accomplishment.

The tally for their work was $13,000. This amount was to be put in a fund for the future first Cody Barrasse Scholar.

So, I was wrong … I truly was comforted, just like the bowl of soup promised.

Soup's on!

Soups

1. Chicken Soup

Inspired by me … Once again, I created this recipe out of desperation when I needed to get a pot of soup ready in a hurry. It became one of my family's favorites.

Total time: 45 minutes
Serves: 12–14 as a first course

Ingredients

1 rotisserie chicken, all meat shredded
(Do not discard carcass.)
3 carrots
3 stalks celery
1 large onion
extra-virgin olive oil
100 ounces chicken broth of your choice (or use more depending on what consistency you like)
3 tablespoons Italian seasoning (or more to taste)
pepper
1/2 cup grated Parmesan cheese
8 ounces small pasta, such as mini farfalle

Directions

Mince celery, carrots, and onion in a food processor.

Sauté vegetables in several tablespoons of extra-virgin olive oil. Add garlic when vegetables are soft and sauté another 30 seconds.

Add broth, shredded chicken, chicken carcass, Italian seasoning, and pepper.

Simmer 30 minutes.

Add Parmesan and simmer 10 more minutes.

Cook pasta separately.

When it's time to serve, place a few spoonfuls of pasta in a bowl and then cover with soup.

You can add more cheese at the time of serving if desired.

2. Chicken Tortilla Soup

The kids are always interested in something Mexican. This is a winner.

Inspired by Add a Pinch.

Total time: 40 minutes
Serves: 6–8

Ingredients

6–8 boneless, skinless chicken thighs
1 (10-ounce) can enchilada sauce
1 (28-ounce) can crushed tomatoes
1 medium onion, diced
4 cloves garlic, minced
2 cups chicken stock

1 teaspoon cumin
1 teaspoon chili powder
1/2 teaspoon sriracha (optional)
1/2 teaspoon kosher salt
1 teaspoon pepper
1 (12-ounce) bag frozen corn

Garnish (Optional)
tortillas
fresh cilantro, chopped
avocado
sour cream
Monterrey Jack cheese, shredded

Directions

Slow Cooker
Place chicken on the bottom of a slow cooker insert. Pour enchilada sauce and crushed tomatoes over the chicken. Add remaining ingredients, except garnish ingredients, and stir together with a spoon.

When slow cooker has finished cooking, shred chicken with two forks and serve with optional toppings.

Stove
Cut the chicken into 3/4-inch pieces and set aside.

Add onion, garlic, and spices to a 6-quart Dutch oven or heavy stockpot set over medium heat. Cook until the onion is tender and the spices fragrant, about 3 minutes.

Stir in the chicken, enchilada sauce, crushed tomatoes, chicken stock, and corn.

Cook until the chicken is cooked through, about 30 minutes.

3. Italian Wedding Soup

Inspired by Damn Delicious.

Total time: 40 minutes
Serves: 4

Wedding Soup is another traditional Italian dish often served on a holiday … and at a wedding!

Ingredients

For the Meatballs

1/2 pound ground chicken (I often use beef.)
1/2 pound chicken sausage, casing removed (I often use sweet Italian sausage.)
1/3 cup panko bread crumbs
1/4 cup grated Parmesan cheese
1 large egg
1/2 teaspoon dried oregano
1 teaspoon dried basil
1/4 teaspoon garlic powder
kosher salt and black pepper to taste

For the Soup

2 tablespoons extra-virgin olive oil, divided
3 cloves garlic
1 onion, diced
3 carrots, diced
2 stalks celery, diced
1/2 teaspoon dried thyme
8 cups chicken stock
2 bay leaves
1/2 cup uncooked acini di pepe pasta
1 sprig rosemary
4 cups baby spinach
1 tablespoon fresh lemon juice
2 tablespoons chopped fresh parsley
pepper to taste
1/4 cup grated Parmesan cheese

Directions

In a large bowl, combine ground meat, sausage, panko, Parmesan, egg, oregano, basil, and garlic powder. Season with salt and pepper to taste. Using a wooden spoon or clean hands, stir until well combined.

Roll the mixture into 3/4-inch meatballs, forming about 25–30 meatballs.

Heat 1 tablespoon extra-virgin olive oil in a large stockpot over medium heat. Add meatballs in batches and cook until all sides are browned, about 2–3 minutes. Transfer to paper towel.

Add remaining 1 tablespoon extra-virgin olive oil to pot. Add garlic, onion, carrots, and celery. Cook, stirring occasionally, until tender, about 3–4 minutes. Stir in thyme and cook until fragrant, about 1 minute.

Whisk in chicken stock and bay leaves and bring to boil. Stir in acini di pepe, rosemary, and meatballs. Reduce heat and simmer until pasta is tender and meatballs are cooked through, about 9–12 minutes.

Stir in spinach and lemon juice until spinach has wilted, about 2 minutes. Season with salt and pepper to taste.

Serve immediately with additional Parmesan.

4. Slow Cooker Beef Barley Soup

Inspired by the Chunky Chef.
This traditional soup is made very simple by using a slow cooker. It warms you up on a cold winter day.

Prep time: 15 minutes
Total time: 6 hours, 15 minutes
Serves: 6–8

Ingredients

1 1/2 pounds beef chuck roast, cut into 1-inch pieces
1–1 1/2 pounds potatoes, peeled and diced into 1/2-inch pieces (Yukon Gold or russet are preferred)
2 carrots, cut into 1/2-inch pieces
1 medium onion, diced
2 ribs celery, diced
4 cloves garlic, minced
2 tablespoons tomato paste
2 tablespoons bouillon base (optional but recommended)
2 teaspoons Worcestershire sauce
1/2 teaspoon kosher salt
1/4 teaspoon black pepper
4 sprigs rosemary
2 bay leaves
6 cups reduced-sodium beef broth
2/3 cup pearl barley

Directions

Heat vegetable oil in a large skillet over medium-high heat. Add beef cubes and brown for 1–2 minutes per side.

Add beef and all other ingredients to a slow cooker and stir to combine.

Cover and cook on low for 7–8 hours or high for 4–5 hours.

Remove bay leaves and thyme stems.

5. Spicy Crab Bisque

Inspired by *Food and Wine*.

Who doesn't like crab?! This is a filling and comforting soup. It's great because it can be made well in advance.

Total time: 45 minutes
Serves: 4

Ingredients

4 tablespoons unsalted butter
1 small white onion, finely chopped
6 celery ribs, finely chopped
6 scallions, thinly sliced
4 bay leaves
1/4 cup flour
5 cups low-sodium chicken broth
2 tablespoons mashed roasted garlic
3 cups whole milk
2 tablespoons dry sherry
1 tablespoon ketchup
1 teaspoon tomato paste
1/4 teaspoon sweet smoked paprika
1/8 teaspoon cayenne pepper
pinch ground cloves
pinch ground mace
pinch nutmeg
1 cup heavy cream
1/2 tablespoon hot pepper sauce
salt
freshly ground pepper
2 pounds jumbo lump crabmeat
oyster crackers for serving

Directions

In a large soup pot, melt butter.

Add onion, celery, scallions, and bay leaves and cook over medium heat until softened, 5 minutes.

Stir in the flour and cook, stirring for 2 minutes.

Gradually whisk in the chicken broth and bring to boil.

Simmer, stirring occasionally, until the broth is thickened and the vegetables are very thickened, 15 minutes.

Add the roasted garlic and milk until thickened. Bring to a simmer.

Stir in sherry, ketchup, tomato paste, paprika, cayenne, cloves, mace, cream, and red pepper sauce and bring to a simmer.

Season with salt and pepper to taste and then add the crab.

Simmer until hot. Remove bay leaves.

Serve with oyster crackers.

This bisque can be refrigerated for up to three days without the crab. Reheat the bisque gently and then add crab just before serving

6. Stuffed Cabbage Soup

Inspired by Patti Morgan.

Patti is another of my friends who come each month to honor Cody. Her son Michael has been one of Cody's dearest friends. She loves to cook and does it very well. You will see many of her recipes scattered throughout this book, and all are worth trying.

Total time: 40 minutes
Serves: 10

Ingredients

4 tablespoons extra-virgin olive oil
1 cup raw white rice
1 quart plus 2 cups chicken stock
1 1/2 pounds ground meatloaf mix plus 1/2 pound ground beef
1/2 teaspoon allspice
2 teaspoons smoked paprika
1 teaspoon salt
1 teaspoon pepper)
1 bay leaf

1 onion, chopped
2 cloves garlic, minced
2 carrots, thinly sliced with a vegetable peeler into strips and then finely chopped
1 small head Savoy cabbage, thinly sliced
1 (28-ounce) can diced tomatoes
1 (15-ounce) can tomato sauce
splash of white vinegar
1 cup cooked rice

Directions

Heat a deep pot over medium heat. Add extra-virgin olive oil.

Once hot, add meat and begin to brown, 2–3 minutes.

Season the meat with allspice, coriander, paprika, salt, and pepper.

Add bay leaf, onions, garlic, and carrots.

Cook vegetables 2–3 minutes to begin to soften them and then add cabbage and wilt it down a bit.

Add tomatoes, tomato sauce, vinegar, and stock and then cover the pot.

Raise the heat to high and bring soup to a simmer. Simmer for 10 minutes.

Add cooked rice and simmer an additional 2–3 minutes.

Add additional salt and pepper to taste.

7. Summer Minestrone

Inspired by *Cooking Light*.
Total time: 65 minutes
Serves: 8

Ingredients

2 tablespoons extra-virgin olive oil
2 cups thinly sliced leeks, white and green parts only
  (about 2 leeks)
1 cup thinly sliced carrots
1 cup thinly sliced celery
3 cloves garlic, minced
2 tablespoons tomato paste
8 cups low-sodium chicken stock
1 (14.5-ounce) can diced tomatoes, undrained
1 (14.5-ounce) can cannellini beans, drained and rinsed

2 cups chopped yellow squash
2 cups chopped zucchini
1 cup chopped red pepper
1 cup fresh green beans, cut into 1-inch pieces
1/2 cup uncooked ditalini pasta
3/4 teaspoon kosher salt
1/2 teaspoon black pepper
5 ounces spinach
1/4 pesto (can be store-bought)
1/2 cup grated Parmesan cheese

Directions

Heat a large pot over medium heat. Add oil, swirling to coat.

Add leeks, carrots, garlic, and celery. Cover and cook 5 minutes, stirring occasionally (do not brown).

Add tomato paste. Cook 2 minutes, stirring constantly.

Add stock and tomatoes and bring to boil.

Reduce heat to low and simmer 15 minutes.

Place 1 can cannellini beans in a small bowl and mash with a fork.

Add mashed beans, squashes, bell pepper, green beans, pasta, salt, and pepper to pot.

Increase heat to medium and cook 10 minutes.

Stir in spinach and cook an additional 2 minutes

Place 2 cups of soup into eight bowls and top each with 1 1/2 teaspoons pesto and 1 tablespoon Parmesan.

8. Black Bean Pumpkin Soup

Inspired by Joe and Kathy DelSerra.

Joe and I have been friends since our days in college at the University of Scranton. He *loves* soup, and he and his wife, Kathy, have passed on several of their superb recipes. This one is a winner.

Total time: 50 minutes
Serves: 8

Ingredients

3 (15.5-ounce) cans black beans, drained and rinsed
1 cup canned diced tomatoes
1 1/4 cup diced onion
1/2 cup shallots
4 cloves garlic, minced
1 tablespoon plus 2 teaspoons cumin
1/2 teaspoon salt
1/2 teaspoon pepper
1/2 stick butter
4 cups beef broth
1 (16-ounce) can pumpkin puree
1/2 cup sherry
1/2 pound ham, diced (optional)

Directions

Puree beans and tomatoes.

Sauté butter, onion, shallots, garlic, cumin, salt, and pepper.

Stir in puree of beans and tomatoes.

Add broth, pumpkin, and sherry. Simmer for 25–30 minutes.

Add ham and 3–4 extra tablespoons of sherry if desired (in place of ham, diced pancetta can be used).

9. Cherry Soup with Lemon Sorbet

Inspired by *Cold Soups* by Nina Graybill and Maxine Rapoport, 1988.

This is one of my favorite summer soups. It's magnificently refreshing and can also be served at the end of dinner as a sort of dessert.

Total time: 3 hours (2 hours for chilling)
Serves: 4

Ingredients

1 1/2 pounds sweet cherries, pitted
1 cup dry red wine
1 cup water
1 tablespoon light brown sugar
1/4 cup plus 2 tablespoons sour cream
3 tablespoons fresh lemon juice
1/2 teaspoon almond extract
4 rounded tablespoons lemon sorbet
4 mint sprigs for garnish

Directions

In a medium saucepan, bring the cherries, wine, water, and brown sugar to a boil.

Reduce heat to low and simmer for 10 minutes.

Let cool for 15 minutes and then puree in a food processor.

Cover the soup and refrigerate until cold, at least 2 hours or overnight.

Add sour cream, lemon juice and almond extract to cherry soup and whisk until smooth.

Ladle soup into bowls and top with the lemon sorbet.

Garnish with mint

I have served this without the sorbet and still enjoyed it.

10. Chicken Miso Soup with Ramen Noodles

Inspired by ratherbeswimmin on Food.com.

Miso gives us that delightful Asian touch, and the ramen noodles bring us back to college days!

Total time: 50 minutes
Serves: 6

Ingredients

3 tablespoons sesame oil
1 bunch scallops, thinly sliced, white and green parts separated
2 tablespoons minced fresh ginger
1 tablespoon minced garlic
6 cups low-sodium vegetable broth (I have also used chicken broth.)
1/3 cup white or red miso
8 ounces shredded rotisserie chicken
1 cup canned sliced bamboo shoots, drained
1 cup canned baby corn, drained
1/2 cup shredded carrot
1 (3-ounce) package ramen noodles, seasoning packet discarded
2 cups baby spinach

Directions

Heat oil in a large saucepan over medium-high heat.

Add scallion whites, ginger, and garlic. Cook mixture until it begins to brown, about 3 minutes.

Add broth and simmer about 10 minutes.

Pour 1 cup warm water into a small bowl. Whisk in miso until dissolved.

Stir miso mixture back into saucepan, decrease heat to medium-low, and keep broth at a simmer.

Stir in chicken, bamboo shoots, corn, carrot, and noodles. Cook until chicken and vegetables are heated through and noodles are tender, 3–5 minutes.

Off heat, stir in spinach.

Garnish each serving with scallion greens.

11. Chipotle Chicken and Corn Chowder

Inspired by Brown Eyed Baker.

There are *so* many types of corn chowder. This one has a little kick to it.

Total time: 1 hour
Serves: 6–8

Ingredients

1 can chipotle chilies in adobo sauce
2 tablespoons unsalted butter
1 poblano pepper, seeded and finely chopped
1 teaspoon cumin
1 teaspoon dried oregano
1/2 teaspoon dried thyme
6 cloves garlic, minced
2 tablespoons flour
3 cups whole milk
2 cups chicken stock

6 small red potatoes, peeled and diced small
4 ounces Monterey Jack cheese, shredded (about 1 cup)
4 ounces cheddar cheese, shredded (about 1 cup)
2 cups diced cooked chicken
1 (30-ounce) can sweet corn, drained
1 (15-ounce) can creamed corn
1 cup crushed tortilla chips
juice from 1 lime
chopped cilantro (garnish)

Directions

Remove one chili from the can of chilies and mince it. Remove 1 teaspoon adobo sauce and set aside to be used later.

Melt the butter in a large pot over medium heat. Add the poblano pepper, red pepper, the chili from the can, cumin, thyme, and oregano and sauté for 5-7 minutes, or until the peppers become soft.

Add the garlic, stir, and cook for 30 seconds, or until fragrant.

Stir in the flour with a wooden spoon and cook for 1 minute, or until there is no longer any visible flour.

Slowly stir in the milk and chicken broth, scraping up any bits from the bottom of the pan as you stir.

Add the potatoes, bring the mixture to a boil, and then reduce the heat to low and simmer for 10–15 minutes, or until the potatoes are tender.

Add the shredded cheeses, a handful at a time, stirring after each addition until the cheese is completely melted.

Finally, stir in the chicken, both cans of corn, tortilla chips, lime juice, and reserved 1 teaspoon of adobo sauce. Cover and cook for an additional 10 minutes, or until soup is completely heated through. Serve immediately.

12. Chorizo Soup

Inspired by Ingrid Beer.

I saw this recipe in a magazine. I do not remember which one, but Ingrid Beer was the author, so I thank her for her absolutely delicious soup. It's one of the kids' favorites.

Total time: 40 minutes
Serves: 6

Ingredients

avocado oil
1 (9-ounce) package pork chorizo, casings removed
2 leeks (white parts only), cleaned, quartered, and sliced
salt
black pepper
6 cloves garlic, minced
1/2 teaspoon ground cumin
1/2 teaspoon chili powder
1/2 teaspoon smoked paprika
1 large sweet potato, peeled and diced
1 (28-ounce) can diced, fire-roasted tomatoes, drained of juice
2 (15-ounce) cans navy beans, drained and rinsed
6 cups chicken stock
2 cup baby spinach
1 tablespoon fresh chopped cilantro

Directions

Place a large soup pot over medium heat and drizzle with 1 tablespoon oil.

Once the pot is hot, crumble in the chorizo and stir for a few minutes until mostly cooked through.

Add the leeks plus a pinch of salt and pepper. Cook for 4 minutes, or until they start to become tender.

Add garlic and stir. Once aromatic, add the cumin, chili powder, and smoked paprika. Stir to combine.

Add in diced sweet potato, the drained fire-roasted diced tomatoes, and the navy beans, along with the chicken stock. Stir to incorporate.

Bring soup to a vigorous simmer.

Cover with the lid ajar.

Turn down the heat and simmer for about 20 minutes, or until the sweet potato is tender.

Turn off the heat and add salt and pepper to taste.

Stir in spinach and cilantro before serving.

13. Corn Chowder

Inspired by *Epicurious*.

This is a great soup to make when corn is bountiful at the end of summer.

Total time: 1 1/4 hours
Serves: 8

Ingredients

1/2 cup diced slab bacon (2 ounces)
2 cups diced sweet onion
2 large carrots, diced into 1/4-inch pieces
1 celery rib, diced into 1/4-inch pieces
1 red bell pepper, dices into 1/4-inch pieces
1/2 pound Yukon Gold (2 small) potatoes, peeled and diced
5 cups reduced-sodium chicken broth
2 fresh thyme sprigs
3 cups corn
1 1/2 cups heavy cream
1/2 teaspoon fine sea salt
1 teaspoon black pepper
fresh chives for garnish
2 plum tomatoes, diced for garnish

(For all of the vegetables, except the potatoes, I use a food processor to dice.)

Directions

Cook bacon in a wide 6- to 8-quart heavy pot over medium heat, stirring frequently until crisp, about 5 minutes.

Transfer with a slotted spoon to paper towels to drain. Add onion, carrots, celery, and bell pepper to bacon fat and cook until onion is softened, 8–10 minutes.

Add the potatoes, broth, and thyme and simmer, covered, until potatoes are just tender, about 15 minutes.

Add sea salt and pepper to taste and then stir in bacon.

14. Julia's Watermelon Gazpacho

Inspired by Allrecipes.
This is a very refreshing starter for a warm summer night. And it could not be healthier!

Total time: 40 min
Serves: 8

Ingredients

6 cups cubed, seeded watermelon
2 English cucumbers, chopped
2 red bell peppers, chopped
1 onion, chopped
1/2 jalapeño pepper, finely chopped
1/4 cup fresh lemon juice
2 tablespoons olive oil
4 tablespoons chopped fresh mint
2 tablespoons minced ginger
3 tablespoons honey
1/2 cup pineapple juice
20 small mint leaves for garnish

Directions

Working in batches, place the watermelon, cucumbers, red bell peppers, onion, jalapeño pepper, lemon juice, olive oil, 3 tablespoons fresh mint, ginger, honey, and pineapple juice into a large pot.

Use immersion blender to be well blended, being sure to retain some texture.

Pour mixture into a large bowl or soup terrine and refrigerate for at least 1 hour. Can be refrigerated overnight.

Serve with mint leaves

15. Lentil Soup

Inspired by Martha Stewart.

Lentil soup is one of those basic go-to soups that's always great on a cold fall or winter day, but it also works in summer. This recipe is simple and scrumptious. Enjoy with a good piece of crusty bread.

Total time:1 hour
Serves: 4

Ingredients

3 strips bacon, cut into 1/2-inch pieces (You can substitute diced pancetta.)
1 large onion, chopped
3 medium carrots, cut into 1/4-inch half-moons (I dice mine in the food processor.)
3 stalks celery, chopped (optional)
3 cloves garlic, minced

2 tablespoons tomato paste
1 1/2 cups lentils, rinsed
1/2 teaspoon dried thyme
2 (14.5-ounce) cans reduced-sodium chicken broth
2 tablespoons red wine vinegar
salt and pepper to taste
grated Parmesan for garnish

Directions

In a large pot, cook bacon over medium-low heat until browned and crisp, 8–10 minutes.

Pour off all but 1 tablespoon of fat.

Add onion, carrots, and celery (if using). Cook until soft, about 5 minutes.

Stir in garlic and cook until fragrant, about 30 seconds.

Stir in tomato paste and cook 1 minute

Add lentils, thyme, broth, and 2 cups of water. Bring to a boil.

Reduce to simmer. Cover and cook lentils until tender, 30–45 minutes.

Stir in vinegar, salt, and pepper.

Serve immediately. I serve with some grated Parmesan.

16. Manhattan Clam Chowder

Inspired by Patti Morgan.

Total time: 45 minutes
Serves: 8

Ingredients

3 stalks celery, chopped
3–4 carrots, chopped
6 potatoes, diced
2 medium onions, chopped
1 stick butter, melted
1 (51-ounce) can clam juice plus 1 (15-ounce) bottle clam juice
1/2 cup dried (or fresh) parsley
1 tablespoon dried oregano
1 teaspoon salt
1 teaspoon pepper
1 (28-ounce) can crushed tomatoes
1 (51-ounce) can chopped clams
1 package frozen peas
1 package frozen corn
2 teaspoons Old Bay Seasoning (optional)

Directions

In a large pot melt butter and add all vegetables and clam juice. Cook until potatoes are tender, about 20–25 minutes

Add parsley, oregano, salt, pepper, and crushed tomatoes. If you are using Old Bay, add it now.

Add chopped clams, peas, and corn.

Bring to boil and then shut off the stove and cover for 5 minutes.

Serve immediately.

17. New England Clam Chowder

Inspired by Delish.

This soup is what Cody craved when he was sick with a cold or flu. One of his favorites.

Total time: 1 hour
Serve: 4

Ingredients

4 slices bacon, cut into 1/2-inch piece
2 tablespoons butter
1 onion, chopped
2 stalks celery, chopped
3 cloves garlic, minced
1/4 cup flour
2 russet potatoes

1 (8-ounce) bottle clam juice
1 cup half-and-half
1 cup vegetable broth
1 bay leaf
4 sprigs thyme
2 (6.5-ounce) cans chopped clams
oyster crackers for serving

Directions

In a large pot over medium heat, cook bacon until crispy. Drain bacon on paper towel, leaving the bacon fat in the pot.

Add butter and allow to melt and then add onion and celery. Cook until tender, about 5 minutes.

Stir in garlic and flour and cook until the garlic is fragrant and the flour turns pale golden, about 1 minute.

Add the clam juice, vegetable broth, and half-and-half, whisking constantly until combined.

Stir in potatoes and bring to a boil and then reduce heat and simmer until potatoes are tender, about 10 minutes.

Add clams and cook until heated through, about 2 minutes. Season chowder with salt and pepper to taste. If the chowder is too thick, gradually stir in more half-and-half until you reach desired consistency.

Garnish with bacon and chives and serve immediately with oyster crackers.

18. Posole (Pork and Hominy Soup)

Inspired by *The Electric Pressure Cooker Cookbook*.

This is a great recipe for Cinco de Mayo! I do mine on top of the stove and simply cook it longer. I love my pressure cooker, but when cooking for twenty-five, I just need a bigger pot.

Total time: 2 1/2 hours
Serves: 6

Ingredients

2 tablespoons vegetable oil
1/2 teaspoon salt plus more as needed
1 1/4 pounds boneless pork shoulder, cut into 4-inch pieces
1 medium onion, chopped
4 cloves garlic, minced
2 tablespoons chili powder
1 quart reduced-sodium chicken broth
2 tablespoons cornstarch
1/4 cup cold water
2 (29-ounce) cans hominy, drained
diced avocado for serving
limes for serving

Directions

In a large pot, heat 1 tablespoon of oil. Season pork with salt and add to heated oil. Cook 5 minutes, browning on all sides. Transfer to a large bowl.

Add the remaining 1 tablespoon of oil to the pot. When hot, add onion, garlic, and chili powder. Sauté for 4 minutes, or until soft.

Stir in 2 cups chicken broth to deglaze the pot, scraping up any brown bits with a wooden spoon. Add the remaining 2 cups chicken broth and the pork. Bring to a boil and then simmer with the lid on for 1 hour, or until pork is falling apart.

Transfer pork to a bowl and shred it using two forks.

In a small bowl, whisk the cornstarch and cold water until smooth.

Add the slurry to the pot and simmer until broth thickens.

Stir in shredded pork and hominy.

Season with salt to taste.

Serve with avocado and lime

19. Peaches and Cream Soup

Inspired by *Cold Soups*.
This is another great soup to refresh and cool us off in the summer.

Total time: 6 hours (including chilling time)
Serves: 6

Ingredients

1 1/2 cups water
1/4 cup sugar
1 (3-inch) cinnamon stick
8 whole cloves
8 peppercorns
6 allspice berries or 1/4 teaspoon ground allspice
2 cups chardonnay
3 pounds very ripe peaches, peeled and pitted, or 2 (10- ounce) packages frozen peaches, thawed
    with juice
1 cup crème fraîche or sour cream
1 heaping tablespoon brown sugar

Directions

In a saucepan, stir together the water, sugar, and spices. Bring to a gentle boil and then cover and simmer for about 30 minutes.

Strain out spices and return syrup to saucepan after cooking.

Meanwhile, puree peaches in a processor until almost smooth. Cover tightly with plastic wrap and set aside.

Add wine to spiced sugar syrup and simmer, uncovered, about 5 minutes. Cool and then stir in pureed peaches.

Refrigerate several hours or up to two days.

Before serving, combine crème fraîche and brown sugar. Ladle soup into bowls and top with generous dollop of the crème fraîche.

20. Potato Soup

Inspired by Gimme Some Oven.

Great for celebrating Saint Patrick's Day!

Total time: 35 minutes
Serves: 6–8

Ingredients

5 slices bacon, diced
1 cup diced white or yellow onion
4 cloves garlic, minced
1/4 cup flour
2 cups chicken or vegetable broth
2 cups milk, warmed
1 1/2 pounds Yukon Gold potatoes, diced
1 cup shredded sharp cheddar cheese
1/2 cup plain Greek yogurt or sour cream
1/2 teaspoon salt, or more to taste
1/2 teaspoon freshly ground black pepper

Optional toppings:
thinly sliced scallions
chives
extra shredded cheese
bacon
sour cream

Directions

Heat a large pot over medium-high heat.

Add diced bacon and cook until crispy, stirring occasionally.

Transfer bacon to a separate plate, using a slotted spoon, reserving about 3 tablespoons of bacon grease in the pot.

Add onion and sauté 5 minutes until soft.

Stir in garlic and sauté an extra 1–2 minutes, stirring occasionally until fragrant.

Stir flour into mixture and sauté for an extra 1 minute to cook flour, stirring occasionally.

Then stir in the stock until combined, followed by the milk and potatoes.

Continue cooking until the mixture just reaches a simmer.

Before it begins to boil, reduce heat to medium-low, cover, and simmer for 10–15 minutes, or until potatoes are soft. Stir often so that bottom does not burn.

Once the potatoes are soft, stir in cheddar and Greek yogurt (or sour cream), salt, pepper, and cooked bacon bits. Taste and season with additional salt and pepper if desired.

Serve warm with garnishes of choice. You can refrigerate for up to three days.

21. Ribollita

Inspired by Bertolli.

This is a classic Italian bread soup. It's very comforting and is filled with great vegetables.

Total time: 45 minutes plus time to refrigerate
Serves: 8

Ingredients

1/4 cup extra-virgin olive oil plus more for serving
1/4 cup chopped trimmed fennel
1/4 cup chopped celery
1/4 cup chopped onions
1/4 cup chopped carrots
1 clove garlic, minced
1/4 teaspoon dried thyme
6 cups chicken broth
1 (28-ounce) can plum tomatoes, cut up (can also use crushed or diced tomatoes)

2 cups peeled and diced russet potatoes
1 1/2 cups drained and rinsed cannellini beans
1 cup finely shredded savoy cabbage
1 cup diced zucchini
3 tablespoons parsley and basil (fresh)
salt and pepper to taste
8 slices 1/2-inch thick Italian bread
grated Parmesan cheese (optional)

Directions

Combine oil, fennel, celery, onions, carrots, garlic, and thyme in a large heavy pot. Cover and cook over medium-low heat until vegetables are very soft, about 15 minutes. Do not brown.

Stir in the broth, tomatoes, potato, beans, and cabbage. Heat to boiling and then reduce heat to low and simmer for 15 minutes.

Add zucchini, parsley, and basil. Cover and cook for 2 minutes. Add salt and pepper to taste.

Remove from heat. Refrigerate for 24 hours.

Just before serving, heat to boiling.

Place a piece of bread in each bowl and drizzle with a little oil.

Ladle soup over bread.

I also add Parmesan to the soup during the last step and at serving time.

22. Roasted Butternut Squash and Pear Soup

Inspired by Flavor the Moments.

This is a classic fall soup. The pears add a touch of sweetness. You will make it over and over again.

Total time: 1 hour
Serves: 8

Ingredients

4–5 tablespoons extra-virgin olive oil
4–5 cups butternut squash cut into 1-inch cubes (about 1 medium butternut squash)
1 1/2 pounds Bartlett pears, peeled, cored, and quartered
1 medium onion, chopped
4 cups low-sodium chicken or vegetable stock
2–4 tablespoons pure maple syrup
1 tablespoon freshly grated ginger
1/4 cup dry sherry (optional)
salt to taste
Greek yogurt or crème fraîche for topping
crystallized ginger for topping
chopped parsley for topping

Directions

Preheat oven to 400 degrees F.

Toss butternut squash with 2 tablespoons oil on a rimmed baking sheet and roast 20 minutes.

Remove from the oven, add pear, and toss gently to coat with the olive oil. Roast for an additional 20 minutes or until softened and caramelized.

Remove from heat.

In a large pot, heat remaining the remaining tablespoon of oil over medium heat. Add onion and cook until softened and translucent, about 5–7 minutes.

Place the squash, pear, onion, broth, 2 tablespoons of maple syrup, and ginger in the pot and use immersion blender until smooth.

Add remaining 2 tablespoons maple syrup and sherry.

23. Sausage and Tortellini Soup

I made this in a pinch when I received unexpected company. I just love this recipe and make it when I need a pick me up.

Total time: 30–40 minutes
Serves: 8

Ingredients

2 pounds ground Italian sausage
2 cloves garlic
3 carrots, shredded
1 large bag spinach
2 (14-ounce) cans fire-roasted diced tomatoes
1 bag cheese tortellini
3 quarts chicken broth
2 tablespoons oregano
black pepper to taste
Parmesan cheese to taste

Directions

Sauté sausage in pot with 1 tablespoon extra-virgin olive oil

When browned, add garlic and cook for 30 seconds, until fragrant.

Add chicken broth, shredded carrots, and tomatoes.

Deglaze pot.

Bring to a boil and then add tortellini, oregano, pepper, and spinach and simmer for 10 minutes.

Add several tablespoons of Parmesan.

Serve immediately.

24. Shrimp Soup with Chili Tortilla Strips

Inspired by *Better Homes and Gardens*.

Total time: 45 minutes
Serves: 6

Ingredients

1 large poblano pepper, seeded and chopped
1 medium onion, chopped
2 cloves garlic, minced
1 tablespoon vegetable or olive oil
1 quart reduced-sodium chicken broth
1/4 teaspoon salt
1/4 teaspoon crushed red pepper
1 (12-ounce) package frozen shrimp, peeled and deveined
1 cup frozen corn
1 (15-ounce) can cannellini beans, drained and rinsed
1/4 cup chopped fresh cilantro
3 tablespoons lime juice
1 small avocado, sliced or chopped
1 batch Chili Tortilla Strips (recipe to follow)

Directions

In a 4- to 5-quart Dutch oven or large pot, cook poblano pepper, onion, and garlic in hot oil until just tender.

Add broth, salt, and crushed red pepper. Bring to a boil.

Add frozen shrimp, corn, and beans. Return to boiling.

Lower heat and simmer, uncovered, about 2 minutes or until shrimp are opaque.

Stir in cilantro and lime juice.

Serve in shallow bowl with avocado and Chili Tortilla Strips

Chili Tortilla Strips

6 (8- or 9-inch) flour tortillas
1 tablespoon vegetable oil

1/2 teaspoon chili powder

Preheat oven to 350 degrees F.

Brush one side of 8- or 9-inch flour tortillas with vegetable oil.

Sprinkle with 1/2 teaspoon chili powder.

Using a pizza wheel, cut into strips or wedges.

Place in a single layer on a very large baking sheet.

Bake 12–15 minutes, or until crisp.

25. Slow Cooker Chicken Enchilada Soup

Inspired by Gimme Some Oven.
This is another great soup for Cinco de Mayo … Or anytime you are in the mood for some fun Mexican food!

Prep time: 10 minutes
Cook time: 4 hours
Serves: 4–6

Ingredients

1 pound boneless chicken breasts (I prefer boneless thighs.)
2 cups chicken stock
1 (10-ounce) can red enchilada sauce
2 (14-ounce) cans black beans, drained and rinsed
1 (14-ounce) can fire-roasted diced tomatoes
1 (15-ounce) can whole kernel corn, drained
1 (4-ounce) can diced green chilies
1 clove garlic, minced
1 onion, diced
1 teaspoon cumin
1/2 teaspoon salt, or to taste

Optional Garnishes
cilantro
avocado
red onion
shredded cheese
sour cream
tortilla chips

Directions

Add all ingredients to a large slow cooker and stir to combine.

Cook for 3–4 hours on high heat or 6–8 hours on low heat until chicken is cooked though and shreds easily.

Use two forks to shred chicken.

Serve warm with optional garnishes.

This can be refrigerated for five days and frozen for up to three months.

26. Crock Pot Chai Pumpkin Soup

Inspired by Barbi Lynch.

Barbi is one of those special women who has been coming to our dinners these past one hundred months. A real friend, she has added so many great foods to our table. She can frequently be found holding a great big wooden spoon, ready to make the pasta.

Prep time: 10 minutes
Cook time: 4 hours
Serves: 4

Ingredients

1/2 cup chopped onion
1 1/2 teaspoons minced garlic
2 teaspoons olive oil
3 cups chicken broth
1 (28-ounce) can unsweetened pumpkin puree
1/4 cup brown sugar
2 chai-flavored tea bags
1/4 cup heavy cream
salt to taste
pepper to taste

This can be easily doubled.

Directions

Place the onion, garlic, and oil in a small bowl and microwave, stirring occasionally until the onion is softened, about 3 minutes.

Scrape the onion mixture into the slow cooker.

Add the broth, pumpkin puree, sugar, and tea bags to slow cooker. Cover and cook until flavors meld, 4–5 hours on low.

Remove tea bags.

With an immersion blender, blend until smooth. Blend in the cream and heat through, about 5 minutes.

Season with salt and pepper to taste.

Chapter 3:

Greens, Grains, and More

A salad is a mixture of chopped food with at least one raw ingredient.

Raw can mean uncooked, but it can also refer to a person who is both untrained and without experience.

The kids fit the definition of raw. They had *no* training or experience in running an organized event as they just had. This eager bunch of kids did it. They managed to pull it off. There were some rough and raw spots during that first tournament, but the kids were reassured that they could make another great tournament happen again. Preparation for the second tournament started shortly after counting the money from the first.

Now the question was: How can we make it better? (And hopefully bigger.) It was time to think outside the box. The first tournament taught us that so many people were willing to help and that so many people wanted to be part of what we represented.

Several within the community simply wanted to be involved. With Michael's guidance, a larger list of potential sponsors was created, and a professional was hired to do some marketing. Eye-catching posters seemed to be everywhere, and the sponsor list was distributed. Then we crossed our fingers.

At the next few dinners, several conversations took place about the energy from that very first tournament. It was clear from the kids, and especially Joseph, that the tournament needed a space to continue this positive energy into the evening. We needed a gathering place. We needed a watering hole.

Eric Shrive, one of Penn State's leading linemen while Cody was in college, owned a bar and restaurant called The Vault. He generously donated his space, as well as a selection of appetizers, and hosted a beautiful event to follow the tournament. Because of his kindness, dozens enjoyed an evening together to relive the day, to savor great company, and to honor their beloved friend.

The second tournament exploded with more than eighty teams. This time, many new faces joined, and some returned with their competitive spirit—just like Cody's—to try to win again.

More merchandise was sold, different shirts were worn, and the number 8 was every place we looked.

Many of the wrinkles of the first year's event were ironed out. Some new ones were identified.

The evening at The Vault gave the day a sense of completion. It was one more way for everyone, but especially the kids, to connect and take pride in what they had just accomplished. Cody was still missing, but they were determined to not let this world forget him.

The great news was that the kids raised enough money to choose the first Cody Barrasse scholar. That scholar would start the following August as a freshman at Scranton Prep. Mission accomplished!

Little did these kids know that their journey was just beginning. They had so much more to do.

The salad was done. The rawness had passed, and now it was on to the main courses.

1. Panzanella

I have been making this for so long that I have no idea who taught me about it. It is, without a doubt, my favorite salad, and it was certainly a favorite of both my sons. It's really a salad of peasants but is magnificently elegant. Use good extra-virgin olive oil and vinegar, and you will not stop smiling.

Total time: 10 minutes
Serves: 4

Ingredients:

8 Campari tomatoes
1 cup fresh mozzarella balls
fresh basil
garlic
salt
pepper
extra-virgin olive oil
balsamic vinegar
crunchy Italian bread or baguette
3–4 tablespoons grated Parmesan, Asiago, or Locatelli cheese

Directions:

Cut ripe tomatoes into bite-size pieces, at least six pieces for each tomato.

Add fresh mozzarella balls.

Shred basil to your liking, at least 5 tablespoons.

Add kosher salt, pepper, olive oil, and balsamic vinegar.

Let salad sit while making the rest of dinner.

In an ovenproof pan, sauté 2–3 cloves of minced garlic until golden.

Add bread to pan and toast until golden.

Place pan in the oven for 5 minutes, or until bread is browned but not burnt.

Add bread to tomato mixture.

Sprinkle with Parmesan, Asiago, or Locatelli.

Tada!

2. Chicken Caesar Salad

Another recipe that was conceived out of desperation. I used what I had on my shelves, and all was well.

Prep time: 5–10 minutes (not counting grill time)
Serves: 6-8

Ingredients

2 hearts romaine lettuce, chopped
3 grilled chicken breasts (marinated in Italian dressing), cut into pieces
2 carrots, shaved
1/2 pint cherry tomatoes, cut in half
Caesar dressing to taste
salt
pepper

Directions

Mix all ingredients together and enjoy.

3. Salad with Cinnamon Apples

I had this at a luncheon one fall afternoon. It's excellent for an autumn salad.

Total time: 10 minutes
Serves: 6

Ingredients

1 bag spring mix salad
1/2 cup cranberries
1/2 cup glazed walnuts
2 Granny Smith apples, sliced and tossed in cinnamon
poppy seed dressing to taste

Directions

Mix all above ingredients together and enjoy.

4. Perfect Winter Salad

Inspired by Taste of Home.

When tomatoes are not very flavorful in the winter, the dried cherries and maple syrup create a perfect salad.

Total time: 20 minutes
Serves: 12

Ingredients:

1/4 cup reduced-fat mayonnaise
1/4 cup maple syrup
3 tablespoons white wine vinegar
2 tablespoons minced shallot
2 teaspoons sugar
1/2 cup canola oil
2 (5-ounce) packages spring mix salad
2 medium tart apples, thinly sliced
1 1/2 cups dried cherries
1 cup pecan halves
1/4 cup thinly sliced red onion

Directions:

In a small bowl, mix first six ingredients and gradually whisk oil until blended. Cover and refrigerate until serving.

To serve, place remaining ingredients into a large bowl and toss with dressing.

5. Hearty Greek Barley Salad

Inspired by Rachel Ray.

This is truly a hearty salad. It can certainly be a great lunch as well as a side salad.

Cook Time: 50 minutes
Prep Time: 15 minutes
Servings: 4

Ingredients:

1 cup pearl barley
salt to taste
pepper to taste
1 cup crumbled feta
1/4 cup extra-virgin olive oil
4 tablespoons red wine vinegar
2 heads romaine lettuce, chopped
2 small cucumbers, such as Persians, chopped
1 cup grape or cherry tomatoes, halved
2/3 cup fresh dill
1/2 cup kalamata olives, pitted
1/2 small red onion, very thinly sliced

Directions:

In medium saucepan with a lid, cook the barley in salted water according to the package directions. Rinse in cold water to cool.

Transfer to a large bowl and season with salt and pepper.

Meanwhile, in a blender, puree 1/2 cup feta with oil and vinegar. Season the dressing.

Toss the barley with the dressing and the remaining ingredients.

6. Winter Italian Chopped Salad

Inspired by *Epicurious*.

The combination of flavors in this powerful salad will make it a family favorite.

Prep time: 45 minutes
Cook time: 45 minutes
Serves: 4–6

Ingredients:

4 tablespoons fresh orange juice
3 tablespoons red wine vinegar
1 large clove garlic, finely grated
1 tablespoon chopped oregano
1 teaspoon Dijon mustard
1/2 cup + 2 tablespoons extra-virgin olive oil plus more for drizzling, divided
1 1/4 tablespoons kosher salt, divided
1/2 pound marinated artichoke hearts (about 1 1/2 cups), drained
4 ounces mini pepperoni rounds
2 (15.5-ounce) cans chickpeas, drained, rinsed, and dried
1/2 head iceberg lettuce, cut into 1-inch pieces (about 8 ounces)
1/2 head radicchio, cut into 1-inch pieces (about 3 ounces)
4 stalks celery, thinly sliced
2 navel oranges, peel and pith removed, cut into 1/2-inch pieces
1/2 pound provolone cheese, cut into 1/2-inch pieces
1 cup pitted black olives, thinly sliced

Directions

Preheat oven to 450 degrees F.

Whisk orange juice, vinegar, garlic, oregano, mustard, 1/4 cup oil, and 3/4 tablespoon of salt in a large bowl.

Toss artichokes, pepperoni, chickpeas, and 2 tablespoons oil on a rimmed baking sheet.

Roast, tossing halfway through, until chickpeas are deep golden brown and pepperoni is crisp, 18–20 minutes.

Add iceberg lettuce, radicchio, celery, oranges, cheese, and olives to bowl with dressing and toss to combine.

Add chickpea mixture to salad and toss again to combine.

Drizzle with more oil before serving.

7. Arugula, Pine Nuts, and Parmesan

Inspired by Food.

This simple salad is just a perfect complement to any dinner.

Total time: 10 minutes
Servers 4

Ingredients

Salad
6 cups leafy arugula
1/2 cup toasted pine nuts
1/4 cup raisins
1/2 cup shaved Parmigiano-Reggiano cheese

Dijon Mustard Vinaigrette (makes 1/3 cup)
1/2 shallot, roughly chopped
1 tablespoon Dijon mustard
2 teaspoons cider vinegar
1/4 cup olive oil
1 teaspoon sugar
juice from 1/2 lemon
kosher salt to taste
fresh ground pepper to taste

Directions

Combine all dressing ingredients in a blender and blend until emulsified and frothy.

Toss all salad ingredients together.

Dress with vinaigrette before serving.

8. Ramen Noodle Salad

Inspired by Dole.

I just love this salad! I love the crunch, and the seasoning packets add an interesting and fun taste.

Total Time:30 minutes
Serving Size: 10

Ingredients

2 (3-ounce) packages chicken-flavored ramen noodles with seasoning packets
1 (14-ounce) bag coleslaw mix
1 (15-ounce) can mandarin oranges, drained
4 green onions, thinly sliced diagonally
8 ounces dried cranberries
12–16 (2/3 cup) snow peas, cut diagonally into thirds
1/2 cup sliced almonds, divided
1/2 cup vegetable oil
1/3 cup sugar
1/4 cup white vinegar

Directions

Preheat oven to 325 degrees F.

Open packages of ramen and remove and discard one seasoning packet. Reserve second packet for dressing. Break up ramen noodles into small pieces.

Arrange noodles on ungreased baking sheet and bake 10–13 minutes, or until lightly browned. Place on wire rack to cool.

Combine coleslaw, mandarin oranges, cranberries, green onions, snow peas, 1/4 cup of almonds, and cooled noodles in a large bowl.

Whisk oil, sugar, vinegar, and reserved seasoning in small bowl until well blended. Pour over the coleslaw mixture and toss to coat evenly. Sprinkle remaining 1/4 cup of almonds over salad.

Note: make 1–2 hours ahead and refrigerate for softer noodles.

9. Mediterranean Farro Salad

Prep time: 15 minutes
Cook time: 30 minutes
Serves: 4

Ingredients

10 ounces farro (about 1 1/2 cups)
1 teaspoon kosher salt plus 1/2 teaspoon, divided
8 ounces green beans cut into 1/2-inch pieces (about 2 cups)
1/2 cup pitted black olives
1 medium red pepper, cut into thin strips (about 4 ounces or 1 cup)
3 ounces Parmesan cheese, crumbled (about 3/4 cup)
1 small bunch chives, snipped (about 1/4 cup)
1/4 cup sherry vinegar
1/4 cup extra-virgin olive oil
1 tablespoon Dijon mustard
1 teaspoon freshly ground black pepper

Directions

In a medium saucepan, combine 4 cups of water with the farro. Bring to a boil over high heat.

Cover and simmer over medium-low heat until farro is almost tender, about 20 minutes.

Add 1 1/2 teaspoons of the salt and simmer until the farro is tender, about 10 minutes longer. Drain well and then transfer to a larger bowl to cool.

Meanwhile, bring a medium pot of salted water to a boil over high heat.

Add green beans and stir. Cook for 2 minutes.

Transfer the cooked green beans to a bowl of ice water and let cool for 2 minutes. Drain the green beans.

Once the farro has cooled, add the green beans, olives, red pepper, Parmesan, and chives. Stir to combine.

In a small bowl, mix together the sherry vinegar, olive oil, mustard, pepper, and remaining 1/2 teaspoon of salt. Stir to combine.

Pour the sherry vinaigrette over the farro salad. Toss to combine and serve.

10. Mexican Grilled Shrimp Caesar Salad

Inspired by *Real Simple*.

Although not a Caesar salad in the true sense, this is a fabulous way to start a meal, especially on Cinco de Mayo!

Total time: 20 minutes
Serves: 4

Ingredients

1/2 cup pepitas (hulled pumpkin seeds)
1 1/2 pounds large shrimp, peeled and deveined
1/4–1/2 teaspoon cayenne pepper
5 tablespoons olive oil, divided
kosher salt
black pepper
1 tablespoon wine vinegar
1 teaspoon Worcestershire sauce
1/4 jalapeño pepper, finely chopped
1 clove garlic, finely chopped
6 cups torn romaine lettuce
1/2 small jicama or 1 Granny Smith apple, cut into matchsticks
1/2 small red onion, thinly sliced
1/2 cup crumbled cotija cheese, queso fresco, or feta cheese

Directions

Heat oven to 350 F degrees.

Spread the pepitas on a rimmed baking sheet and toast in oven, tossing once, until fragrant, about 6–8 minutes.

Heat grill to medium-high.

In medium bowl, toss the shrimp with the cayenne, 1 tablespoon of olive oil, 1/2 teaspoon of salt, and 1/4 teaspoon pepper. Grill until opaque throughout, 2–3 minutes per side.

In a large bowl, combine vinegar, Worcestershire sauce, jalapeño, garlic, remaining 4 tablespoons olive oil, and 1/4 teaspoon each of salt and black pepper. Add the lettuce, jicama, onion, pepitas, and shrimp and then toss to combine. Sprinkle with cotija.

11. Arugula, Watermelon, and Feta Salad

Inspired by Food Network and Ina Garten.

What a refreshing summer salad with a great combination of flavors.

Total time: 10–15 minutes
Serves: 4

Ingredients

1/4 cup freshly squeezed orange juice
1/4 cup freshly squeezed lemon juice (2 lemons)
1/4 cup minced shallots (1 large)
2 tablespoons honey
1/2 cup extra-virgin olive oil
1 teaspoon kosher salt
1/2 teaspoon freshly ground black pepper
6 cups baby arugula, washed and spun dry
1/8 seedless watermelon, rind removed and cut into 1-inch cubes
12 ounces good feta cheese, diced into 1/2-inch cubes
1 cup (4 ounces) whole, fresh mint leaves, julienned

Directions

Whisk together the orange juice, lemon juice, shallots, honey, salt, and pepper. Slowly pour in the olive oil, whisking constantly, to form an emulsion. If not using within an hour, store the vinaigrette covered in the refrigerator.

Place the arugula, watermelon, feta, and mint in a large bowl. Drizzle with enough vinaigrette to coat the greens lightly and toss well. Taste for seasoning and serve immediately.

12. Greek Salad with Farro

Inspired by the Dietitians from Regional Hospital in Scranton.

I found this recipe in the coffee shop at the hospital one summer day. Farro adds a special twist for a great salad.

Total time: 10 minutes
Serves: 6–8

Ingredients

Salad
1 cup farro
1 cucumber, peeled and diced
1 red pepper, diced
1/2 cup chopped red onion
1/4 cup fresh dill, minced
1/4 cup fresh mint, chopped
1/2 cup crumbled feta cheese

Vinaigrette
- 3 tablespoons red wine vinegar
- 1 clove garlic, minced
- 1/2 teaspoon kosher salt
- 1/4 cup olive oil

Directions

Place rinsed farro in a large saucepan and cover with 2 quarts of salted water. Bring to a boil.

Reduce heat and simmer, uncovered, for about 30–35 minutes. (Farro will have a similar texture to barley when cooked.) Drain it well and set aside to cool completely.

Whisk together vinaigrette ingredients.

Place all the salad ingredients, including the cooled farro, in a bowl and toss with vinaigrette. Serve at room temperature or chilled.

13. Fattoush, Mixed Herb, and Toasted Pita Salad

Inspired by *Cooking Light*.

This is a classic Middle Eastern salad. The special ingredient is sumac. I use both the sumac and lemon as well as the juice from the lemon.

Total time: 15 minutes
Servings: 4 (2 cups each)
Note: Ground sumac is available at Middle Eastern markets.

Ingredients

2 (6-inch) pitas
3 tablespoons ground sumac or 3 tablespoons grated lemon rind
1 tablespoon extra-virgin olive oil
8 cups thinly sliced romaine lettuce
2 cups chopped tomatoes
1 1/2 cups chopped fresh parsley
1 cup thinly sliced green onion
1/2 cup chopped mint
1/2 teaspoon salt
1 cucumber, quartered lengthwise and thinly sliced (about 2 cups)

Directions

Preheat oven to 400 F degrees.

Place pitas on a single layer on a baking sheet. Bake for 6 minutes or until toasted.

Break into bite-size pieces.

Combine pita, sumac, and oil, tossing well to coat.

Add lettuce and remaining ingredients and toss well.

14. Mixed Citrus Green Salad

Inspired by MyRecipes.

Citrus is a nice alternative to our traditional salads. The dressing really gives it life.

Total time: 10 minutes
Serves: 6–8

Ingredients

1 1/2 cup red seedless grapes, halved
2 (5-ounce) bags mixed greens
1 (11-ounce) can mandarin oranges
1 (8-ounce) container red grapefruit, drained
7 tablespoons Orange Poppy Seed Dressing (recipe to follow)
1 cup walnut halves, toasted

Directions

Combine first 5 ingredients in a large bowl.

Arrange 2 cups salad on seven plates and drizzle each with 1 tablespoon Orange Poppy Seed Dressing, or to taste).

Top with walnuts.

15. Orange Poppy Seed Dressing

Yield: 1 cup plus 2 tablespoons (1 tablespoon serving size)

Ingredients:

1/2 cup fresh orange juice
1/4 cup honey
1/4 cup canola oil
3 tablespoons champagne vinegar
1/8 teaspoon salt
1 teaspoon poppy seeds

Directions:

Combine first five ingredients in a blender and process until blended. Add poppy seeds and pulse once.

Cover and refrigerate.

16. Spinach Salad with Hot Bacon Dressing

Inspired by Laurie Quinn.

Ingredients

Salad
baby spinach leaves
hard-boiled eggs
sliced mushrooms
sliced red onion

Dressing
6 slices bacon, diced
1/3 cup cider vinegar
3 tablespoons sugar
2 tablespoons water
1/4 teaspoon salt
1/4 teaspoon dry mustard

Directions

In a skillet over medium heat, cook bacon until browned. Remove bacon from skillet.

Pour off all but 1/4 cup drippings.

Add vinegar and other ingredients to bacon drippings and cook and stir until sugar is dissolved.

Add bacon.

Mix with spinach, eggs, onion, and mushrooms.

17. Aunt Meg's Special Salad

Inspired by my longtime friend known as Aunt Meg by my children. She was taken from us much too soon but left her mark on us permanently.

Total time: 10 minutes
Serves: 8–10

Ingredients

1 large container spring mix
2 cans mandarin oranges
1 cup craisins
1 cup glazed walnuts, chopped
1 1/2 cups sliced strawberries
1 cup cherry tomatoes, halved
1 cup blue cheese, crumbled
raspberry vinaigrette to taste
kosher salt
pepper

Directions

Mix all ingredients together.

Season with salt and pepper to taste.

Chapter 4:

Pasta, Pasta, and More Pasta

Pasta is any flour and egg preparation that creates an unleavened dough to be produced in a variety of shapes.

Dough is soft. It can be pasty, but it is always pliable.

Sometimes it's flat.
Sometimes it's round.
Sometimes it's a tube.

You can never make too much pasta.
You can eat it for breakfast.
You can eat it for lunch.
You can eat it for dinner or a midnight snack.

You can heat it up in the microwave.
Or simply eat it cold.
You can eat it from a china plate.
Or even a big plastic bowl.

To Cody, pasta was one of the four basic food groups. It absolutely sustained him. It comforted him, and it gave him the energy to imagine the impossible and think beyond what was usually expected.

Fast-forward to spring of 2015. The kids had two tournaments under their belts, with the second being even more successful than the first. The happy hour at The Vault made it clear just how important it was to be together after the tournament. But there was still something missing.

As the kids thought about our purpose, they realized two things. First, it was time to start the arduous process of becoming our own nonprofit organization—in the world of the IRS, a 501(c)(3). They were clueless about the task, but they quickly caught on. They knew that this would take some time, but they needed to start somewhere. Second, they realized that a memorial three-on-three basketball tournament where hundreds could play honoring Cody was terrific, but it was simply not enough.

Cody was a hero—in life and in death. He truly gave everything he had away. On his twenty-second birthday several weeks before he died, we had a brief, yet very intense conversation about some of his strong feelings. He made it very clear that if anything ever happened to him that prevented him from living life as he currently was, he wanted to be fully let go and instructed me to give everything he had away. The conversation was not morbid. It was very matter-of-fact. I had no idea where this conversation came from, and I tried to explain to Cody that he would be making those decisions for me, not me for him. He made me promise. And I did.

Little did I know that Cody had an identical conversation with his brother, Joseph.

I just can't make this up.

So, when we realized that Cody could not survive his injuries, the decision to proceed with organ donation was easy. It was what Cody wanted. It was that simple.

It became clear to the kids and Joseph that we needed to spread this message: the message of ultimate courage, selflessness, and love. This led to the decision to create an evening event solely devoted to organ donor awareness and to spread the message of the miracle of organ donation and transplantation.

This was no small task. We needed a venue. We needed food. We needed music. We needed a grand plan.

With the help of a few senior mentors, the kids figured it out.

They found a place to hold five hundred people. They found twenty venders to donate a wide variety of fabulous foods. They found others to donate beverages. They found a band.

Yes, there were a lot of moving parts.

The marketing piece exploded. There were billboards and a website, and finally the pieces started to connect.

We called the evening event, Continue Cody's Commitment: A Night to Promote Organ Donor Awareness.

We had no idea how this night would turn out. We prayed to have two hundred people attend. That night on the floor of a ballroom built in the 1920s, the room was packed. The line to get inside was out the door, and the energy was palpable. The excitement was loud, and the music was happy.

And then came the video.

We felt strongly that there needed to be a moment during this great evening of remembrance to tell Cody's story and talk about the importance of organ donation. The video was going to make our event more than just a party.

The music stopped, and Joseph spoke to the crowd. And then there was silence. A massive screen showed pictures of Cody from his childhood until his death. These were melded with touching and powerful words from Joseph about his brother. There were also stories from those among us who received transplants.

The quiet was deafening. The message was clear. There were tears. But more importantly, there was a greater sense of determination of how necessary this mission really was. The world, at least our small piece of the world in northeastern Pennsylvania, had been ignited to become organ donors and to spread our story. Mission accomplished—again.

The kids, along with their senior mentors, were like dough. They were not afraid to be pliable or to reshape themselves to make a better event.

That night, I went home weary after a very long, yet magnificent day. It was sometime after midnight, and I had myself a bowl of cold pasta in memory of my precious Cody.

1. Bolognese Sauce

Inspired by my Mom.

There are many versions of this classic sauce. This is the recipe as I was taught. It can be used on its own over a ridged pasta. I also use it as my sauce for my lasagna.

Total time: 1 1/2 hours
Serves: 8–10

Ingredients

4–5 tablespoons extra-virgin olive oil
1 pound ground beef
1 pound ground pork
1 pound ground Italian sausage (mild or hot)
3–4 carrots, diced
2 onions, diced
4–5 cloves garlic, minced
1 cup red wine
4 cans crushed tomatoes
3 (15-ounce) cans tomato paste
45 ounces water
8–9 sprigs fresh rosemary
1 handful dried fennel
1 handful dried oregano
salt to taste
pepper to taste
1 cup heavy cream
2–3 handfuls grated Parmesan cheese

Directions

In a large pot, heat olive oil and brown beef, pork, and sausage. Sauté in batches. When brown, remove from pot and set aside in a large bowl.

In the drippings, sauté chopped carrots, celery, and onion until soft. Add garlic and cook until fragrant, about 1 minute.

Deglaze the pot with red wine, scraping up all the browned bits. Then put the browned meat back into pot.

Add crushed tomatoes, tomato paste, and water. Mix thoroughly.

Add rosemary, fennel, oregano, salt, and pepper. Cook for 10 minutes.

Add cheese and heavy cream. Cook for 1 hour or so. If it is too thick for your liking, add more water.

Serve over a pasta with ridges.

2. Shrimp and Scallop Sauce

This was one of Cody's (and his friends') favorites. I needed something for dinner one night, and this is what happened. Hungry kids will do it to you.

Total time: 30 minutes
Serves: 4–6

Ingredients

1 pound medium shrimp, deveined and peeled
1/2 pound bay scallops
1 stick butter
8 ounces sun-dried tomato paste
8 ounces prepared pesto
3 cloves garlic, minced

juice from 1 lemon
1/4 cup white wine
black pepper to taste
salt to taste
3–4 tablespoons grated Parmesan cheese

Directions

Melt butter in large pan.

Sauté garlic until fragrant, about 30 seconds.

Add shrimp and scallops. Cook until shrimp are pink and scallops are opaque.

Add sundried tomato paste and pesto.

Add lemon juice and white wine. Stir.

Add black pepper and salt. Simmer 5–10 minutes.

Sprinkle in a handful of Parmesan and simmer another 3–5 minutes

Serve over your choice of pasta. I use linguini.

Add more Parmesan

(There is a longstanding battle about serving cheese with fish sauces. The only place in Italy that allows this is in Sicily. Since I am Sicilian, it's OK!)

3. Shrimp Scampi Pasta

Inspired by *Epicurious*.

This is an easy go-to meal. It can be used as a weeknight dinner or for a fancy dinner party. I always have a bag of frozen shrimp in my freezer … just in case

Total time: 20 minutes
Serves: 4

Ingredients

1/4 cup olive oil
1 pound large shrimp (20–25 per pound), peeled and deveined
6 cloves garlic, minced
1/2 teaspoon red pepper flakes
1/2 cup dry white wine
1 teaspoon salt
1/2 teaspoon black pepper
5 tablespoons unsalted butter
3/4 pound angel-hair pasta
1/2 cup parsley, chopped

Directions

Bring a 6- to 8-quart pot of salted water to boil.

Heat oil in a large skillet over medium-high heat until hot but not smoking.

Sauté shrimp, turning over once, until cooked through, about 2 minutes. Transfer to a large bowl with a slotted spoon.

Add garlic to oil remaining in the skillet along with red pepper flakes, wine, salt, and pepper. Cook over high heat, stirring occasionally, 1 minute.

Add butter to skillet, stirring until melted, and then stir in the shrimp.

Remove from heat.

Cook pasta in boiling water until just tender. Reserve 1 cup pasta water and then drain pasta using a colander.

Toss pasta well with shrimp mixture and parsley. Add some pasta water if necessary to keep moist.

4. Simple Alfredo Sauce

Inspired by Aunt Janine, my friend for more than thirty years. She is a great cook, a great friend, and a great aunt to my boys.

This sauce is a big hit with the kids. It's certainly not a low-fat recipe, but it is fabulous.

Ingredients

1 stick butter
4 cups heavy cream (1 quart)
4 ounces cream cheese, cut into small chunks
2 cups (or more) grated Parmesan cheese to thicken sauce to your liking
2 tablespoons minced garlic
salt to taste
pepper to taste
garlic salt to taste
fresh Italian parsley, chopped

Directions

In a medium saucepan, heat butter on low heat and sauté minced garlic.

Add heavy cream and whisk constantly until it begins to bubble.

Add one piece of the cream cheese at a time to the sauce. Make sure to keep whisking to avoid burning the bottom.

Add cheese a handful at a time. Use as much or as little as you like.

Season with salt, pepper, garlic salt, and parsley. Simmer until sauce thickens, about 30 minutes.

Serve over pasta of your choice and top with grated cheese and parsley

5. Bacon and Tomato Linguini

Inspired by Food Network.

This is a BLT in a bowl over pasta.

Total time: 25 minutes
Serves: 4

Ingredients

12 ounces linguini
6 slices bacon, cut into 1/2-inch pieces
3 cups cherry or grape tomatoes
1 shallot, thinly sliced
2 large eggs
1/2 cup grated Parmesan cheese plus
    more for topping
2 teaspoons finely grated lemon zest
freshly ground pepper
1 cup fresh basil, torn

Directions

Bring a large pot of salted water to a boil. Add the pasta and cook as label directs.

Reserve 1 cup cooking water. Drain pasta. Set aside.

Meanwhile, cook the bacon in large skillet over medium-high heat until crisp, about 5 minutes.

Add tomatoes and shallots and cook until tomatoes burst, about 5 min.

Pour off all but 2 tablespoons bacon drippings.

Whisk the eggs, lemon zest, cheese, and 1 teaspoon pepper in a medium bowl. Slowly whisk in 1 cup reserved cooking water. Set aside.

Reduce the heat under the skillet to medium-low. Add the pasta and toss well. Slowly pour in the egg mixture, tossing to make a creamy sauce, about 1 minute

Season with salt and pepper. Stir in basil. Top with more cheese.

6. Chipotle Chorizo Mac and Cheese

This mac and cheese has a little kick. It's one of my very favorites.

Total time: 45–50 minutes
Serves: 4–6

Ingredients

4 cups whole milk
1/2 cup unsalted butter
1/2 cup all-purpose flour
1 pound elbow macaroni
8 ounces pork chorizo
1 teaspoon kosher salt

1/2 teaspoon pepper
3 chipotles in adobo, diced
8 ounces shredded pepper jack cheese (I used Monterey Jack.)
4 ounces shredded Gouda cheese plus 1/4 cup for topping
1 cup panko bread crumbs
1 tablespoon butter, melted

Directions

Preheat oven to 350 degrees F. Spray 9- x 13-inch baking dish with cooking spray and set aside

In a medium saucepan over medium heat, simmer the milk until it almost comes to a boil and then remove from heat and set aside.

In a large saucepan, melt butter over medium heat. Whisk in the flour and continue to whisk until the butter and flour mixture is a pale blond color, about 3–4 minutes.

Quickly pour the warmed milk in to the flour mixture, whisking constantly until well combined. Continue to whisk the sauce until it's thick and can coat the back of a spoon, about 3 minutes. Remove from the heat and set aside.

In a large pot of boiling salted water, cook pasta to al dente, about 2 minutes less than recommended cooking time. Drain the pasta and run cold water over it to stop the cooking.

Remove chorizo from casing. Cook the chorizo in a small skillet over medium-high heat until browned, 6–8 minutes. Drain on paper towel and set aside.

Place sauce over medium-high heat and stir until warm. Season with salt, pepper, and chipotles and stir to combine.

Add pepper jack and 4 ounces Gouda in handfuls and stir to melt into sauce.

Add the pasta to the sauce and fold in the chorizo. Then pour the mixture into prepared baking dish.

Combine panko and melted butter in a bowl. Top the macaroni with remaining 1/4 cup Gouda and sprinkle with panko topping. Bake 15–20 minutes, until bubbling

7. Grilled Chicken Buffalo Pasta

Inspired by Carrie's Experimental Kitchen.

This recipe is a great one for game day.

Total time: 30 minutes
Serves: 4

Ingredients

2 (6-ounce) boneless chicken breasts, sliced in 1/2 horizontally (I have also used tenders.)
1/2 pound penne pasta
1/2 cup your favorite wing sauce
1/2 cup chunky blue cheese dressing
Italian parsley for garnish

Directions

Cook pasta according to package direction. Drain.

While the pasta is cooking, grill chicken. It can be done on an indoor grill.

Slice chicken breasts diagonally.

Add the cooked pasta to a large bowl along with grilled chicken, wing sauce, and blue cheese dressing. Mix well and serve.

8. Manicotti

Inspired by my old friend Angie.

This is a classic Italian recipe. We serve this on Easter and on Cody's anniversary. This was the last dinner Cody shared with me at Easter dinner 2013—one of his absolute favorites.

The sauce I use for this is what some would call Sunday Sauce. In our house, it is simply a "Pot of Sauce". Make the sauce far in advance.

The manicotti can be frozen on wax paper on a baking sheet. Once frozen, I place them in freezer bags. To serve, defrost and place in a baking dish with sauce.

Total time: 1 hour or so
Makes about 40 manicotti

Ingredients

Crepes
12 eggs
3 1/2 cups flour
3 1/2 cups water

Cheese
1 large container ricotta cheese
2 eggs
salt to taste
pepper to taste
1/4 teaspoon nutmeg
3 tablespoons dried mint
1 teaspoon granulated garlic
4–5 tablespoons grated Parmesan cheese

Directions

For the Cheese Stuffing
Mix all ingredients thoroughly and set aside.

For the Crepes
Mix all ingredients until well blended.

Spray a small frying pan (the size used for omelets) with cooking spray and heat over medium-high heat.

Pour one small ladle full of batter into pan and spread it over the entire pan to achieve the thinnest crepe you can make.

Cook until crepe is firm but not completely browned. They should be soft.

Using a spatula, place crepe on a wax paper–covered surface to cool.

Once cooled, place about 1–2 heaping tablespoons of ricotta mixture in the middle of the crepe.

Roll crepes and place in a glass baking dish (or aluminum pan) that has already been covered with a layer of sauce (pot of sauce).

Place manicotti snuggly in the pan and then cover with more sauce and sprinkle with Parmesan.

Cover and bake in a 350-degree oven for 30 minutes.

9. Pasta with Chicken, Artichokes, Roasted Peppers, and Olives

This is another recipe made out of desperation. Keep the ingredients in your pantry, and you will always be able to make a great dinner.

Total time: 30 minutes
Serves: 4

Ingredients

1 pound chicken tenders, cut into 1-inch pieces
1 bottle marinated artichokes
1 bottle roasted red peppers, cut into slices
1 small can sliced black olives
1 small can peas (or frozen peas)
4–6 tablespoons sun-dried tomato paste
1/2 cup white wine
8 ounces chicken broth
3–4 tablespoons Italian seasoning
black pepper to taste
extra-virgin olive oil
grated Parmesan cheese

Directions

Sauté chicken pieces in extra-virgin olive oil until just about done. Do not overcook.

Add artichoke hearts, roasted red peppers, olives, and peas and stir. Cook about 2–3 minutes.

Add sun-dried tomato paste. Cook together for 5 minutes or so.

Deglaze with white wine. Add broth, Italian seasoning, and pepper.

Simmer about 10 minutes and then add 3–4 tablespoons cheese.

Serve over pasta of your choice. I use linguini or spaghetti, but just about any type will do.

If sauce is too thick, add more broth to make the consistency you like. You can also use reserved pasta water.

10. Patti's Mac and Cheese

Inspired by Patti Morgan.

Mac and cheese is just one of those comfort foods that is irresistible, and Patti's is fantastic!

Total time: 55 minutes
Serves: 6

Ingredients

1 tablespoon olive oil
1 1/2 teaspoons kosher salt
1 pound penne
4 cups whipping cream
16 ounces white cheddar cheese, grated
16 ounces smoked Gouda cheese, grated
2 1/2 tablespoons chopped fresh rosemary
2–3 teaspoons freshly ground pepper

Directions

Preheat oven to 375 degrees F.

Bring 4 quarts of water to a boil. Stir in olive oil, salt, and pasta. Cook accordingly to package. Drain well.

Bring cream to a simmer. Do *not* boil.

Stir in cheddar and smoked Gouda. Add rosemary and stir until well blended. Remove from heat and add pasta.

Pour into greased 3-quart baking dish.

Bake 30–35 minutes or until golden brown.

Let stand 10 minutes before serving

11. Classic Pesto

Inspired by *Bon Appétit*.

When Spring brings us the green leaves and the beautiful grass, my soul yearns for this simple sauce. There is nothing like homemade pesto. Despite the kids' aversion to most things green, they do gobble this one up.

Ingredients

4 cups fresh basil leaves (from about 3 large bunches)
1/2 cup extra-virgin olive oil
1/2 cup pine nuts
3 cloves garlic
1/2 cup grated Parmesan cheese
1 teaspoon kosher salt

Directions

Combine basil, oil, pine nuts, and garlic in a food processor. Blend until paste forms, stopping often to push down basil.

Add cheese and salt and blend until well combined.

Pesto can be made 1 day ahead. Top with 1/2-inch olive oil and chill. It also freezes very well.

When serving with pasta, I warm my pesto gently, not to a boil. If it's too thick, you can add some reserved pasta water to make it the consistency that you like.

12. Pot of Sauce

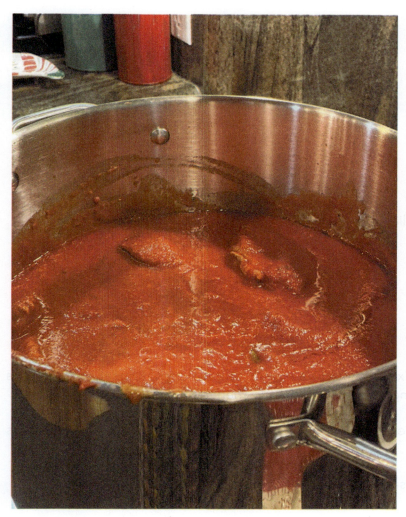

Inspired by my Mom and Aunts who first taught me how to cook.

This type of sauce has had many names. Some call it ragù because it is a sauce with meat. Some call it Sunday Sauce because this is the type of sauce that immigrant Italians served at their traditional Sunday midafternoon dinner, usually with meatballs, sausage, or perhaps beef and pork. Some people, believe it or not, call it gravy. I personally can't figure that one out. Gravy is brown and goes on turkey.

In our home, it was simply called a "Pot of Sauce." Everybody knew exactly what you meant if you said you were making a Pot of Sauce. There are many variations. Some use crushed tomatoes, some whole, some paste. Every family has their own recipe and way of doing it. I have made this sauce thousands of times. It is never exactly the same. Measuring might help, but it's just not something I do very well.

Ingredients

Sauce
1/2 cup red wine
extra-virgin olive oil
4–5 cloves garlic, minced
6 large cans tomato paste
3 (28-ounce) cans of crushed tomatoes
salt to taste
pepper to taste
6–7 sprigs fresh basil, chopped
1/2 cup grated Parmesan cheese

Meatballs
Inspired by my dear friend Rose.

1 cup bread crumbs
1/2 cup warm milk
1/2 pound ground beef
1/2 pound ground pork
2 eggs
1/2 cup grated Parmesan cheese
salt to taste
pepper to taste
2 teaspoons granulated garlic
1 tablespoon dried mint, crumbled

I also include 1 pound sweet or hot Italian sausage links, a few pork ribs, and a piece of chuck.

Directions

For the Meatballs
Preheat oven to 350 degrees F.

Mix all ingredients. Add milk slowly. Mixture should be moist but not sloppy. If meat mixture goes through your fingers easily without leaving much on your hands, then the texture is good.

Roll meatballs and place on a baking sheet. Bake for 20 minutes or until cooked through. The meatballs can also be fried in oil in a frying pan.

Set aside until you're ready to make the sauce.

For the Sauce
Fry sausage links, spare ribs, and chuck in a large pan. Sear meat on all sides.

Remove meat from pan and add one large can of tomato paste to drippings. Fry the paste in the pan and deglaze with 1/2 cup red wine and 3 cans of water. Simmer for 10–15 minutes.

In a large pot, add 1/4 cup extra-virgin olive oil. Sauté 4–5 minced cloves of garlic until golden. Do *not* burn. Remove garlic from oil. Add 6 large cans of tomato paste with 12 cans of water. Stir well. Then add 3 cans crushed tomatoes. Simmer and stir frequently.

Add ingredients in frying pan with drippings to sauce.

Add salt and pepper to taste, chopped basil, and Parmesan. Stir well.

Then add meatballs, sausage, pork, and chuck (if used). Simmer several hours, stirring frequently.

If too thick, add water to make desired consistency

13. Sausage and Pepper Sauce with Cavatelli

Inspired by Patti Morgan.

Sausage and peppers are historically eaten by themselves in a bowl or on a good, crusty Italian roll. This sauce is perfect over a good cavatelli. Homemade are best, but there are many excellent store-bought versions.

Total time: 1 hour
Serves: 8

Ingredients

2 (28-ounce) cans crushed tomatoes
8 cloves garlic, minced
1/4 cup plus 2 tablespoons extra-virgin olive oil
2 teaspoons red pepper flakes
2 1/4 teaspoons kosher salt
1 pound Italian sausage, casings removed and crumbled
1 Vidalia onion cut into thin strips

2 red bell peppers, cut into thin strips
2 yellow bell peppers, cut into thin strips
3 tablespoons red wine vinegar
1 pound cavatelli
1/4 fresh basil, thinly sliced
1 tablespoon chopped fresh oregano
grated Parmesan cheese

Directions

In a large stockpot, add 1/4 cup oil and the garlic.

Cook garlic over medium heat, stirring occasionally, until fragrant, about 2–3 minutes

Stir in tomatoes and reduce heat to low. Simmer 10 minutes.

Stir in the red pepper flakes and 2 teaspoons salt. Set aside.

Heat 1 tablespoon oil in a large frying pan. Add the sausage and cook until browned. Add sausage to tomatoes.

Add onions, peppers, and remaining salt and oil to skillet. Sauté on medium heat. Cook until soft, about 5 minutes.

Add the red wine and cook until the liquid is evaporated, about 2 minutes.

Stir the peppers and onions into the tomato sauce.

Prepare cavatelli according to package directions.

Reserve 1 tablespoon basil for garnish. Fold in oregano, cooked pasta, and remaining basil.

Cook 1 minute to blend flavors. Sprinkle with Parmesan and serve

14. Short Rib and Porcini Mushroom Ragù

Inspired by *Fine Cooking*.

This is a very hearty sauce and is great for a cold winter night. It's the only sauce I make that is made predominantly in the oven.

Yields 8 cups of ragù.

Ingredients

1 ounce dried porcini mushrooms (about 1 cup)
2 (28-ounce) cans crushed tomatoes
1/2 cup extra-virgin olive oil
2 pounds bone-in beef short ribs, trimmed of excess fat
1 pound boneless beef chuck
kosher salt
freshly ground pepper
1 small onion, finely chopped
1 small carrot, finely chopped
1celery stalk, finely chopped
1 clove garlic, minced
4 ounces pancetta, finely chopped
1 tablespoon chopped flat leaf parsley
1 cup dry white wine

Directions

Position rack in lower third of oven and heat oven to 300 degrees F.

Soak mushrooms in 2 cups warm water for 20–30 minutes. With a slotted spoon, transfer mushrooms to a cutting board and chop finely. Strain mushroom-soaking water to remove grit. Put liquid and mushrooms aside.

Heat 1/4 cup oil in a 7- or 8-quart Dutch oven. (I use a large roasting pan.) Season the ribs and chuck with salt and pepper and add them to the hot oil. Cook, turning as needed, until the meat is browned on all sides, about 10 minutes.

Transfer meat to a large platter. Clean pan with paper towels.

Heat the remaining 1/4 cup oil in the pan over medium heat.

Add onion, carrot, celery, garlic, and pancetta and cook, stirring frequently, until vegetables are soft and golden, about 7–8 minutes. Add mushrooms and parsley and stir for 1 minute.

Return meat to pan and stir to coat with savory base. Raise heat to high and add wine. Cook until wine is reduced by half, about 5 minutes.

Add tomatoes and 1/2 cup reserved mushroom soaking water. Season with 1/2 teaspoon salt and 1/4 teaspoon pepper. Stir until liquid begins to simmer.

Cover the pan tightly and put it in the oven. Cook, turning meat every half hour, until meat is fork-tender and ribs begin to fall off the bones, about 2 1/2 hours.

Remove pan from the oven and transfer meat to cutting board. Pull meat off ribs. Discard bones and shred meat.

Stir meat back into sauce and simmer on the stove top to allow flavors to meld, about 10 minutes.

Serve with your favorite pasta. I use pappardelle.

Sprinkle with grated Parmesan.

15. Pasta with Shrimp Fra Diavolo

Inspired by Marie Perry, one of my nurses on Telemetry.

Ingredients

1 pound large shrimp, peeled and deveined
1/2 teaspoon salt
1 teaspoon dried red crushed pepper flakes
3 tablespoons extra-virgin olive oil
1 medium onion, sliced
1 (14-ounce) can diced tomatoes

1 cup dry white wine
3 cloves garlic, minced
1/2 teaspoon dried oregano
3 tablespoons parsley
3 tablespoons dried basil

Directions

Toss shrimp, salt, and pepper flakes. Set aside

Heat oil in large heavy skillet over medium-high heat

Add shrimp and sauté until pink and cooked through, about 1–3 minutes. Transfer to plate and set aside.

Add onion to the same skillet. Add 1–2 teaspoons olive oil and sauté until translucent, about 5 minutes

Add tomatoes and their juice, wine, garlic, and oregano. Simmer until sauce thickens, about 10 minutes.

Return shrimp and any accumulated juices to tomato mixture.

Toss to coat and cook 1–2 minutes.

Stir in parsley and basil. Season with salt to taste and serve over your favorite pasta

16. Sun-dried Tomato Pasta with Chicken and Creamy Mozzarella Sauce

Inspired by Julia's Album.

This dish is truly comfort food. You will leave the table very satisfied and happy.

Total time: 40 minutes
Serves: 4

Ingredients

4 cloves garlic, minced
4 ounces sun-dried tomatoes
1 pound chicken tenders, sliced
1/4 teaspoon salt
1/4 teaspoon paprika
1 cup half-and-half

1 cup shredded mozzarella cheese (Use preshredded, not fresh mozzarella.)
8 ounces penne
1 tablespoon basil
1/4 teaspoon red pepper flakes
1/2 cup reserved pasta water
salt to taste

Directions

In a large skillet, sauté garlic and drained sun-dried tomatoes in 2 tablespoons olive oil for 1 minute on medium heat

Remove sundried tomatoes from skillet. Add sliced chicken (salted and covered with paprika) and cook on high heat for 1 minute on each side. Remove from heat.

Cook pasta according to package instructions. Reserve some of the cooked pasta water and drain pasta.

Slice sun-dried tomatoes into smaller pieces and add them back to skillet with chicken.

Add half-and-half and mozzarella to skillet and bring to gentle boil. Immediately reduce heat to simmer and cook, constantly stirring, until all cheese melts and creamy sauce forms.

Add cooked and drained pasta to skillet with cream sauce and stir to combine.

Add 1 tablespoon basil and 1/4 teaspoon red pepper flakes.

If sauce is too thick, add 1/2 cup reserved water to the skillet.

Season with salt and pepper to taste.

17. Joe's Baked Pasta

Inspired by my incredible friend Joe DeAndrea who has treated me like another daughter. As I write this book, he will be turning ninety-five years old. He is a remarkable chef and an incredible example of determination and spunk. It is impossible to really describe him, and we are blessed to have him in our lives.

Prep time: 1 hour
Cook time: 3 1/2 hours
Serves: 6

For the Bolognese Sauce

Ingredients

3 tablespoons minced onion
3 tablespoons extra-virgin olive oil
3 tablespoons butter
2 ribs celery, chopped
2 carrots, chopped
3/4 pound ground beef

1 cup white wine
1/2 cup milk
salt
1/4 teaspoon nutmeg
2 cups chopped canned tomatoes with juice

Directions

In a deep pot, place extra-virgin olive oil, butter, and onion. Sauté until soft.

Add celery and carrots. Sauté 5 minutes.

Add beef. Cook until not red but do not brown.

Add wine and turn heat up.

Then lower heat and add milk and nutmeg. Cook until evaporated.

Add tomatoes and simmer uncovered for 3 1/2 hours.

For the Bechamel

Ingredients

2 cups milk
4 tablespoons butter

3 tablespoons flour
1/4 teaspoon salt

Directions

In a small pan, heat the milk until it comes to the very edge of a boil.

While heating the milk, melt the butter over low heat in a heavy saucepan that can hold 4–6 cups. When the butter is melted, add all the flour, stirring constantly with a wooden spoon.

Let the flour and butter bubble for 2 minutes, stirring constantly. Do not let the flour become colored.

Turn off heat and add the hot milk 2 tablespoons at a time. Once the milk is incorporated, add another 2 tablespoons milk.

When all milk is incorporated, reduce heat to low, add salt, and stir until sauce is dense as cream.

For the Pasta

1 pound rigatoni
2 cups Bolognese
medium-thick bechamel sauce
6 tablespoons grated Parmesan cheese
2 tablespoons butter

Directions

Preheat oven 400 degrees F.

Cook pasta in boiling salted water until al dente.

Drain pasta and transfer to a large mixing bowl.

Add Meat sauce, the bechamel, and 4 tablespoons grated cheese to pasta. Mix thoroughly.

Transfer to greased baking dish. Level the top with a spatula, sprinkle with remaining 2 tablespoons grated cheese, and dot with butter.

Place in uppermost level of oven and bake 10–15 minutes.

Allow to settle a few minutes before serving.

18. Marinara Sauce

I use the same sauce used in my caponata. It's simple but does the job. I like it with angel-hair pasta.

Total time: 25–30 minutes
Serves: 4

Ingredients

1 (28-ounce) can crushed tomatoes
2–3 cloves garlic, minced
2 sprigs basil (or more to taste)
1/2 cup extra-virgin olive oil
salt
pepper

Directions

Simmer tomatoes with garlic, basil, and oil for 15–20 minutes.

Add salt and pepper to taste.

19. Lasagna

Inspired by *Fine Cooking*.

Lasagna is the quintessential meal for a crowd. This particular recipe has been tweaked multiple times and remains a family favorite. The surprise is that ricotta cheese is not used. The bechamel combined with *lots* of grated Parmesan makes a cheese-like filling that is light and addictive.

Ingredients

1 pot of Bolognese Sauce (recipe is found earlier in this chapter)
3 boxes no-boil lasagna noodles
1 1/2 sticks butter plus more for greasing pan
1 1/2 cups flour
3 cups whole milk
4–5 cups grated Parmesan cheese
1 cup shredded mozzarella

Directions

Heat oven to 400 degrees F. Grease a lasagna pan with butter. (I often use a roasting pan.)

Make the bechamel: Melt butter in a saucepan, whisk in the flour, and cook 2–3 minutes. Pour in the milk, whisking constantly. Cook until it starts to thicken.

Place a thin layer of the Bolognese sauce on the bottom of the pan. Then place lasagna noodles on top of this thin layer Bolognese.

Place a slightly thickened layer of sauce on top of the lasagna noodles and cover with bechamel. This may be thick, and you may have to spread it evenly over the sauce with a spatula.

Sprinkle handfuls of Parmesan over the bechamel. Do not be bashful. Make sure bechamel is thoroughly covered with cheese.

Then start whole process again: noodles, Bolognese, bechamel, cheese.

End with a layer of noodles.

Cover noodles with a thin layer of sauce and sprinkle with more Parmesan and shredded mozzarella.

Bake uncovered for 30 minutes.

Chapter 5:

For the Carnivores

Meat … It is the flesh of an animal that is eaten. It is the substance and center of the meal. It is the entrée.

That's why there are such idioms as "the meat of the matter." They imply the main issue—the real purpose.

The kids had taken another great leap by initiating Continue Cody's Commitment. It helped define what we represented: a daytime filled with healthy competition honoring one of the world's toughest competitors and an evening dedicated to the wonder of organ donation.

The baton was now gradually passed to the stewardship of the kids. The senior mentors gracefully bowed out to leave the strategy and innovation to these steadfast young people.

They were definitely ready. They had their own ideas and opinions. They had the energy. And, mainly, they had an endless devotion and love for Cody. It was now their time to be completely in charge.

Now there were regular meetings with minutes. There were officers, and there was letterhead. The meetings were run under Joseph's tender, yet strong leadership. Each of these young people brought something special to the table, and each had a distinct role within the foundation. There were future lawyers and physicians. Several worked in the world of finance. Others worked in marketing and design and still others in journalism and communications. Some lived close by. Some lived farther away. Yet, they all worked with a single purpose.

This incredible group of determined young adults strategized, discussed, and respectfully argued about the direction that this foundation would take. Dates were set, venues were chosen, and sponsorships were both discussed and sought. The basic idea of who we were as a foundation and what we wanted to accomplish was always at the heart of any discussion.

As the kids matured through this process, it was clear that the concept of organ donation was front and center. Educating a single student every other year changed that student's life journey. Its impact was on a single individual. Educating the world and spreading the invaluable message of the miracle of organ donation, however, was much further reaching. Its boundaries were potentially endless. These kids saw no limits with what they could do. They wanted their message to be global.

So, as time passed and the kids' influence took root, they made a few things crystal clear:

1. Cody would never be forgotten.
2. A deserving scholar would be named every other year to attend Scranton Prep in Cody's name. The scholar would live by the same principles Cody had lived by and represent Cody throughout his or her life.
3. Most importantly, the foundation would transform a tragic event into positive energy by educating as many people as possible about the importance of organ donation.

The mission and vision statements were then written. The kids' voices were heard, and there was not a single question about the foundation's intention. And then, finally, the long-awaited letter came. The letter from the IRS granting us the designation as a real 501(c)(3) arrived. We were now an actual nonprofit organization acknowledged by our federal government. This gave us a great sense of accomplishment, but even more, it gave us a tremendous feeling of permanence.

Our foundation was the real thing and here to stay.

And so, the entrée had been served!

This was like biting into that big, fat steak!

The meat of the matter was clear.

Yet another mission accomplished.

1. Chicken Cacciatore

Inspired by Williams Sonoma.

This is a real comfort food. The sauce the chicken creates is like no other. Enjoy this simple but delicious dish.

Prep time: 20 minutes
Serves: 6

Ingredients

1/3 cup flour
1/2 tablespoon salt plus more for taste
1 1/2 teaspoons ground pepper plus more for taste
8 pieces chicken thighs and legs (with bone and skin)
1/4 cup olive oil
2 red bell peppers, sliced
1 yellow onion, halved and sliced

5 cloves garlic, minced
3/4 cup dry wine
3/4 cup chicken broth
1 (28-ounce) can crushed tomatoes
1 tablespoon dried oregano (or more to taste)
6 ounces cremini mushrooms, sliced (shitake mushrooms also work)

Directions

In a large, shallow bowl, stir together flour, 1 tablespoon of salt, and 1 1/2 teaspoons of pepper.

Coat the chicken pieces evenly with flour, shaking off excess.

In a large frying pan over medium-high heat, warm the oil.

Add chicken pieces, in batches if necessary, skin side down, and cook until golden brown on the bottom, about 7 minutes.

Turn the chicken and cook on the second side until lightly browned, 3–4 minutes more.

Transfer chicken to a slow cooker.

Return the frying pan to medium-high heat.

Add the bell peppers, onions, and garlic and sauté until they start to soften, about 3 minutes.

Pour in the wine and broth and deglaze the pan, stirring to scrape up the browned bits on the bottom of the pan.

Stir in the tomatoes and oregano and bring to simmer. Pour the mixture over chicken.

Cover and cook on high for 4 hours or on low for 8 hours.

About 30 minutes before the dish is ready, stir in the mushrooms and season with salt and pepper to taste.

Serve as it is with crusty bread or over linguini or spaghetti.

2. Greek Chicken

Inspired by *Cook's Country*.

Total time: 45 minutes plus chilling time
Serves: 4

This chicken is packed with flavor! It's crispy on the outside and juicy on the inside. Although this recipe is for four, this dish can easily be made for a crowd.

Ingredients

1/4 cup extra-virgin olive oil
2 tablespoons chopped fresh rosemary
2 tablespoons chopped fresh thyme
6 cloves garlic, minced
lemon zest from 1–2 lemons
1–2 tablespoons lemon juice
1 tablespoon kosher salt

1 1/2 teaspoons dried oregano
1 teaspoon coriander
1/2 teaspoon red pepper flakes
1/2 teaspoon pepper
3 pounds bone-in chicken pieces (I use only chicken thighs.)

Directions

Combine oil, rosemary, thyme, garlic, lemon zest, salt, oregano, coriander, pepper flakes, and pepper in a large bowl.

Cut three 1/2-inch deep slits in the skin side of each chicken thigh.

Transfer chicken to bowl with marinade and turn to thoroughly coat, making sure marinade gets into slits.

Cover and refrigerate for at least 30 minutes or up to 2 hours. (I have marinated this overnight.)

Adjust rack 6 inches from broiler element and heat oven to 425 degrees F.

Place chicken pieces, skin side up, in a 12-inch oven-safe skillet.

Using a rubber spatula, scrape any remaining marinade from the bowl over chicken.

Roast until thighs register 175 degrees, 30–35 minutes

Remove skillet from oven and spoon pan juices over the top of chicken to wet skin.

Heat broiler and broil chicken until skin is lightly browned, about 3 minutes, rotating skillet as necessary for even browning.

Let chicken rest in the skillet 10 minutes.

Transfer chicken to shallow platter. Stir lemon juice into pan juices and then spoon over chicken.

3. Balsamic Chicken with Roasted Vegetables

Inspired by Skinnytaste.

When you talk about simple and efficient, this one says it all. Everything is on one sheet pan, and in a short time, you can have a great and healthy dinner on the table.

Total time: 30 minutes
Serves: 4

Ingredients

8 boneless, skinless chicken thighs
1 teaspoon kosher salt
fresh black pepper to taste
cooking spray
10 medium asparagus spears, ends trimmed
2 red bell peppers, sliced into strips
1 red onion, chopped into chunks
1/2 cup sliced carrots
5 ounces sliced mushrooms
1/4 cup plus 1 tablespoon balsamic vinegar
2 tablespoons extra-virgin olive oil
3 cloves garlic, smashed and roughly
  chopped
1/2 teaspoon sugar
1 1/2 tablespoons fresh rosemary
1/2 tablespoon dried oregano or thyme
2 leaves fresh sage, chopped

Directions

Preheat oven to 425 degrees F.

Season chicken with salt and pepper.

Spray two large baking sheets with oil.

Combine all the ingredients together in a large bowl using your hands to mix well.

Arrange everything onto prepared baking sheets spread out in a single layer.

The vegetables should not touch the chicken, or it will steam instead of roast.

Bake about 20–25 minutes, rotating the pan top to bottom, or until the chicken is cooked through and the vegetables are roasted and tender.

4. Oven-Baked Baby Back Ribs

Inspired by Aunt Janine.

This was Cody's favorite Birthday dinner. He just loved them. And I continue to make it every February to remember how he loved this dish.

There are so many ways to make ribs. This is an easy method that delivers a fabulous meal.

Ingredients

St. Louis-style ribs (1/2 rack per person)
BBQ sauce of your choice
salt

pepper
garlic salt
your favorite dry rub

Directions

Preheat oven to 325 degrees F.

Cut each rack of ribs into thirds and put on a large baking pan.

Season with salt, pepper, and garlic salt. If you wish, you can also rub the meat with your favorite rub at this point.

Place seasoned ribs in a large roasting pan and cover with foil.

Bake for 1 hour or until no longer pink.

Turn the ribs and drain the juice from the pan about halfway through.

Cover the pan and bake for another hour. Drain grease again.

Uncover ribs. Coat with the BBQ sauce and continue baking until ribs begin to brown and BBQ sauce thickens a bit, stirring occasionally.

5. Brisket Alla Natalie

Inspired by my friend Natalie Gelb.

The Friday after Cody was buried, Natalie delivered a beautiful Sabbath dinner. This brisket recipe was her bubbe's (grandmother) recipe. It was so comforting at a time we needed comfort.

All measurements are approximate, so here it goes …

Ingredients

1 (4–5-pound) beef brisket
seasoned salt
kosher salt
pepper
3–4 cloves garlic, minced
2 onions, sliced
1 (28-ounce) can tomato sauce
1 bag small carrots
2 cups crushed ginger snaps (I crush them in my food processor.)
3–4 potatoes, quartered

Directions

Preheat oven to 350 degrees F.

Trim excess (but not all) fat from brisket.

Rub seasoned salt, kosher salt, and pepper over brisket.

Heat a heavy pan over high heat and sear brisket on all sides.

Transfer brisket to a large roaster and surround with onions, carrots, and potatoes.

Spread minced garlic over the top of the meat and then sprinkle with crushed gingersnaps.

Roast for several hours, until very tender, but not totally falling apart.

6. Chicken Enchiladas

Inspired by Taste of Home.

The kids go wild over these. It had to be Cody's influence. He was the king of tacos and enchiladas.

Total time: 1 hour
Serves: 5 (2 per person)

Ingredients

1 (10-ounce) can enchilada sauce (can also use homemade version, recipe to follow) I use more sauce than this and would recommend having at least 2 cans available.
4 ounces cream cheese
2 cups salsa
2 cups shredded chicken (I use rotisserie chicken.)
1 (15-ounce) can pinto beans, drained and rinsed (can also use black beans or kidney beans)
1 (4-ounce) can chopped green chilies
10 (6-inch) flour tortillas
1 cup shredded Mexican cheese blend

Optional Toppings
shredded lettuce
chopped tomato
sour cream
sliced black olives

Directions

Preheat oven to 350 degrees F.

Spoon 1/2 cup enchilada sauce into a greased 9- x 13-inch baking dish.

In a large saucepan, cook and stir the cream cheese and salsa over medium heat until blended, 2–3 minutes. Stir in the chicken, beans, and chilies.

Place about 1/3 cup of chicken mixture down the center of each tortilla.

Roll up and place seam side down over sauce. Top with remaining enchilada sauce and sprinkle with cheese

Cover and bake at until heated through, approximately 25–30 minutes.

Serve with optional toppings if desired.

I also add half enchilada sauce and half salsa inside the tortilla.

Homemade Enchilada Sauce

Ingredients

3 tablespoons olive oil
3 tablespoons flour
1 tablespoon chili powder (scale back if you prefer it not so spicy)
1 teaspoon cumin
1 teaspoon garlic powder
1/4 teaspoon dried oregano
1/4 teaspoon salt
pinch of cinnamon
2 tablespoons tomato paste
2 cups vegetable broth
1 teaspoon apple cider vinegar
ground pepper to taste

Directions

Put all dry ingredients into a small bowl and set near the stove.

In a medium-sized pot over medium heat, warm the oil until hot enough that a light sprinkle of flour sizzles on contact. This might take a few minutes.

Once it is ready, pour in the flour and spice mixture. While whisking constantly, cook until fragrant and slightly deepened in color, about 1 minute.

Whisk the tomato paste into the mixture and then slowly pour in the broth while whisking constantly to remove any lumps.

Raise heat to medium-high and bring mixture to a simmer. Cook, whisking often, for about 5–7 minutes, or until the sauce has thickened a bit and a spoon encounters some resistance as you stir it.

Remove from the heat and then whisk in vinegar and season to taste with black pepper. Add more salt to your taste.

7. Chicken with Roasted Red Pepper Sauce

I have been making this chicken for so long that I have no idea where it came from. It has been a favorite of my family's.

Total time: 45 minutes
Serves: 2–8

Ingredients

2 pounds chicken tenders
flour for dredging
2–3 eggs, beaten with a fork
bread crumbs (panko bread crumbs can also be used)
extra-virgin olive oil
2 jars roasted red peppers, drained
1/2 cup red wine vinegar
1 cup chicken broth
salt
pepper
1/2 cup grated Parmesan cheese
1/2 cup shredded mozzarella

Directions

Pound chicken tenders with a mallet.

Dredge tenders in flour, dip in beaten eggs, and then dredge in bread crumbs.

Repeat process with remaining tenders.

Sauté tenders in oil in a large pan over medium-high heat until both sides are golden. Place cooked tenders on a plate until all are done.

Meanwhile, use a blender to combine roasted peppers, vinegar, and chicken broth.

Transfer all cooked tenders to a baking pan and pour the blended mixture over the chicken.

Cover and cook for 10 minutes.

Sprinkle with both Parmesan and mozzarella, cover again, and cook an additional 5 minutes.

Serve over angel-hair pasta or on its own with a side dish.

8. Chili

I had the only Italian grandmother who could not cook. But she was the *best* gram anyone could have ever had. The week I went off to medical school, she gave me a cookbook that she bought in the equivalent of a dollar store. I treasure the book. Her own handwriting is in it. She certainly *never* used it. I have been making this chili recipe, with a few tweaks, since my early days in medical school, thinking of her each time I make it. I love you, Gram.

Total time: 2 hours
Serves: 16

Ingredients

3 cans red kidney beans
1 can black beans
3 cans crushed tomatoes
3-4 red bell peppers, seeded and sliced
vegetable oil
2 large onions, chopped
3 cloves garlic, minced
3 pounds ground beef

1/3 cup chili powder (back off a bit for those who enjoy a milder form)
2 tablespoons salt
1 1/2 teaspoons pepper
1 1/2 teaspoons cumin
1/2 bag frozen corn
shredded Mexican cheese blend for topping (optional)

Directions

In a large pot, place crushed tomatoes. Add beans and start to warm through.

In a large pan, sauté peppers in 2 tablespoons vegetable oil.

Add onions and cook until soft, stirring frequently.

Add garlic and cook 1 minute.

In another large skillet, brown ground beef.

Add beef to onion mixture.

Stir in chili powder and cook 10 minutes.

Add beef mixture to tomatoes and beans.

Stir in remaining ingredients and then cover and simmer for 1 hour.

Remove cover and continue simmering for 30 more minutes.

Serve as it is or over rice.

You can top each bowl with shredded Mexican cheese blend if desired.

9. Cider-Brined Pork Roast with Potatoes and Onions

Inspired by *Bon Appétit*.

Pork is a symbol of good luck and prosperity at the New Year. So, I love to make this for our January dinner.

Ingredients

1 cup packed light brown sugar
1 cup kosher salt plus more
8 bay leaves, divided
3 tablespoons coriander seeds, divided
1 tablespoon black peppercorns plus more freshly ground
1 quart apple cider
1 (8-bone) pork roast (about 5 pounds), chine bone removed, rib bones frenched, and tied with kitchen twine
6 Yukon Gold potatoes, unpeeled and quartered
4 medium red and/or yellow onions, halved
5 tablespoons olive oil, divided

Directions

Bring brown sugar, 1 cup salt, 2 bay leaves, 1 tablespoon coriander seeds, peppercorns, and 2 cups water to a boil in a medium saucepan. Reduce heat and simmer, stirring occasionally, until sugar and salt dissolve, about 4 minutes.

Transfer brine to a large bowl and add cider and 2 cups of ice. Let cool.

Place pork and brine in a large (2-gallon) resealable plastic bag. Seal bag and chill at least 8 hours.

Remove pork from brine and pat dry with paper towels. Let sit at room temperature for 1 hour.

Toss potatoes and onions with 4 tablespoons of oil in a large roasting pan. Season with salt and pepper and set aside.

Place rack in lower third of oven and preheat to 425 degrees F. Crush the remaining 2 tablespoons of coriander seeds.

Season pork with salt and pepper and rub all over with crushed coriander.

Heat remaining 1 tablespoon of oil in a large skillet over medium-high heat. Cook pork until browned on all sides, 8–10 minutes.

Transfer pork to roasting pan and nestle among the vegetables. Tuck remaining bay leaves under kitchen twine over top of pork.

Wrap bone tips with foil to prevent burning and place in oven to roast, turning vegetables halfway through. Roast until meat thermometer registers 140 degrees, 60–75 minutes.

Remove foil from bones and transfer pork to cutting board.

Let rest 30 minutes before slicing between ribs into chops.

The pork can be brined up to two days ahead and chilled.

10. Fruity Grilled Pork Tenderloin

Inspired by Allrecipes.

Pork tenderloin is perfect for a crowd. And grilling in the summer is a perfect way to prepare it. I had not used black cherry soda for years until I found this recipe. I know you will enjoy it.

Total time: 4 hours, 45 minutes
Serves: 4

Ingredients

1/4 cup soy sauce
1/2 cup packed brown sugar
1/3 cup plum jam

3/4 cup black cherry soda
1 (1-pound) pork tenderloin

Directions

In a small saucepan, mix together soy sauce, brown sugar, and jam over low heat until sugar has dissolved.

Reserve 1/4 cup of sauce for basting the tenderloin while grilling.

Combine remaining sauce with soda in a large plastic bag. Place meat in bag and seal. Marinate for at least 4 hours or overnight.

When you're ready to cook, preheat the grill to medium heat.

Lightly oil the grill and discard marinade. Cook tenderloin for 15–20 minutes, or until a meat thermometer inserted into the center of the tenderloin reads 145 degrees.

Remove meat from grill and allow to rest 5 minutes before slicing into 1/4-inch thick medallions.

11. Grilled Asian Flank Steak with Sweet Slaw

Inspired by *Epicurious*.

Total time: 1 hour
Serves: 4

This is a crowd pleaser. These kids are definitely carnivores and love this flank steak. No matter how much I prepare, they will eat it!

Ingredients

1/4 cup soy sauce
5 tablespoons vegetable oil
5 teaspoons minced fresh ginger, divided
2 cloves garlic, minced
1 (1 1/2-pound) flank steak
3 tablespoons sugar
3 tablespoons seasoned rice vinegar
2 jalapeños, thinly sliced into rounds
5 cups thinly sliced Napa cabbage
3/4 cup chopped green onions, divided

Directions

Prepare grill for medium heat.

Mix soy sauce, 3 teaspoons ginger, and garlic in a resealable plastic bag.

Add flank steak and seal bag; turn to coat. Let stand at room temp for 30 minutes, turning occasionally.

Stir sugar and vinegar in a small saucepan over medium heat until sugar is dissolved. Remove from heat.

Add jalapeños and remaining 2 teaspoons ginger to saucepan.

Place cabbage and 1/2 cup green onions in medium bowl.

Pour vinegar mixture over the cabbage and onions and toss to coat. Season with salt and pepper and let stand while grilling steak, tossing occasionally.

Grill steak until cooked to desired doneness, about 6 minutes per side for medium rare.

Transfer meat to work surface and let rest 10 minutes.

Slice steak thinly against the grain. Serve with slaw.

12. Grilled Honey Lime Cilantro Chicken

Inspired by The Recipe Critic.

The combination of flavors in this recipe makes for a terrific meal. If you prefer chicken with skin, it can be easily substituted. It's simply a great Mexican dish.

Total time: 15 minutes
Serves: 4–6

Ingredients

2 pounds boneless, skinless chicken thighs
1/4 cup lime juice
1/2 cup honey
2 tablespoons soy sauce
1 tablespoon olive oil
3 cloves garlic, minced
1/2 cup cilantro, chopped
1/2 teaspoon salt
1/4 teaspoon pepper

Directions

Put chicken in a ziplock bag.

In a small bowl, combine lime juice, honey, soy sauce, olive oil, garlic, cilantro, salt, and pepper.

Pour the sauce over the chicken and seal the bag.

Marinate for 3 hours or overnight.

When ready to cook, preheat grill to medium-high heat.

Grill each side of chicken for 3–4 minutes or until cooked through and no longer pink

13. Guinness-Glazed Slow Cooker Corned Beef

Inspired by Closet Cooking.

Total time: 8 hours and 30 minutes (5 minutes prep time)
Serves: 12

Northeastern Pennsylvania is steeped in a strong Irish heritage. Everyone is Irish on St. Patrick's Day! This corned beef is frequently the center of attention during our March dinner.

Ingredients

1 (4-pound) corned beef in pickling liquid and spices
12 ounces Guinness or other Irish stout
1 small onion
2 cloves garlic, minced
1/4 cup brown sugar
2 tablespoons grainy mustard
1 tablespoon Worcestershire sauce
salt to taste
pepper to taste

Directions

Place corned beef along with pickling spices, onion, and garlic in a slow cooker with the fat layer on top.

Pour in the Guinness and cook on low until fork tender, about 8–10 hours.

Set the corned beef aside.

Strain the solids from the juices and place the liquid into a large saucepan.

Add brown sugar, mustard, Worcestershire sauce, salt, and pepper. Bring to a boil.

Reduce heat and simmer to reduce by half, about 10 minutes.

Cut the fat layer from the corned beef. Cover with Guinness glaze and bake in a preheated 400-degree oven until glaze starts bubbling, about 10–15 minutes

14. Pesto Chicken Breasts

Inspired by *Great Grilling* by Carol Haddex and Jean Marie Brownson, 1993.

Total time: 1 hour
Serves: 6–8

This is a great summer entrée, full of flavor and easy to prepare. I use chicken thighs, which work very nicely.

Ingredients

1 cup prepared pesto
3 tablespoons seasoned rice vinegar
1 tablespoon Dijon mustard
1 teaspoon coarse ground pepper
1/8 teaspoons cayenne pepper
6 large whole chicken breasts, deboned and split. (I prefer boneless, skinless thighs)

Directions

Combine the pesto, vinegar, mustard, black pepper, and cayenne in a small bowl.

Transfer to a large plastic bag and add the chicken.

Seal the bag tightly and turn it over several times so chicken is well coated.

Refrigerate for 30–60 minutes.

Remove chicken from marinade.

Grill over medium-hot fire, turning once, about 10 minutes.

15. Pulled Pork

This is a very old recipe. I just cannot remember where I got it. My boys loved it. They ate it for lunch, for dinner, and for midnight snacks. I also use this recipe to make pulled pork nachos, which is a great appetizer.

Prep time: 30 minutes
Cook time: 9 hours
Serves: 12

Ingredients

1 (5–6-pound) pork shoulder with bone in
1/2 bottle ketchup
2 cups BBQ sauce
1/2 teaspoons tabasco (or more to taste)
2 tablespoons Worcestershire sauce
several pinches cayenne pepper
1/2 can cola
kosher salt to taste
pepper to taste

Directions

Tightly wrap pork in several layers of aluminum foil.

Place in slow cooker and add 2–3 inches of water.

Cover slow cooker and cook on low for 9 hours, or until pork pulls apart easily.

Remove pork from slow cooker and open foil. Drain juices.

Pull the pork with 2 forks and transfer back to slow cooker.

Add all other ingredients and mix with a wooden spoon.

Heat through about 1 hour on low.

16. Slow Cooker Tacos Al Pastore

This book would not be complete without mention of tacos. From the time Cody was eighteen months old until his passing, there were *always* tacos in the refrigerator. For him, tacos were part of his daily existence. He liked *all* types at *all* times. On his twenty-first birthday, he went to his favorite Taco Bell while at Penn State and had twenty-one tacos and burritos (along with his favorite cocktail).

Prep time: 10 minutes
Cook time: 4 hours
Serves: 6–8

Ingredients

1 (5-pound) boneless pork shoulder (Boston butt), excess fat trimmed
12 ounces beer
2 chipotles in adobo sauce
1 fresh pineapple, peeled, cored, and roughly chopped
1/2 cup chopped red onion
3 tablespoons chili powder
3 tablespoons fresh lime juice
2 tablespoons white vinegar
2 teaspoons kosher salt
1 teaspoon cumin
1/2 teaspoon black pepper
corn tortillas for serving

Optional Toppings
crumbled goat cheese
extra pineapple
chopped cilantro
diced avocado

Directions

Cut the pork shoulder into 2-inch cubes and place in a slow cooker.

Add the chipotles in adobo, pineapple, red onion, chili powder, lime juice, white vinegar, salt, cumin, and black pepper to a blender or food processor. Puree until mixture is completely smooth, 30–60 seconds. Stir in the beer until evenly combined.

Pour the mixture on top of the pork and toss until pork is evenly coated.

Cook on low for 8–10 hours or high for 4–5 hours, until the pork is completely tender and shreds easily with a fork. Use two forks to shred the pork and then toss it in the remaining juices.

Serve warm on tortillas. Garnish with optional toppings.

17. Tacos Carne Asada

Inspired Food Network.

Total time: 2 hours, 10 minutes
Serves: 4 (2 tacos per person)

Ingredients

2 pounds flank or skirt steak, trimmed of excess fat
1 recipe mojo, recipe to follow
olive oil for coating grill
kosher salt
pepper
16 corn tortillas
shredded lettuce
chopped white onion
shredded Monterrey Jack cheese
1/2 cup pico de gallo (recipe to follow)
2 limes, cut in wedges

For the Mojo
5 cloves garlic, minced
1 jalapeño, minced
1 large handful cilantro, finely chopped
kosher salt
pepper
juice of 2 limes
juice of 1 orange
2 tablespoons white vinegar
1/2 cup olive oil

In a mortar and pestle or bowl, mash together the garlic, jalapeño, cilantro, salt, and pepper to make a paste. Put the paste in a glass jar or plastic container.

Add the lime juice, orange juice, vinegar, and oil. Shake it up really well to combine.

For the Pico de Gallo
4 vine-ripe tomatoes, chopped
1/2 medium red onion, chopped
2 green onions, white and green parts, sliced

In a mixing bowl, combine all ingredients together. Toss thoroughly.

Let sit for 15 minutes to an hour to allow flavors to marry.

Directions

Lay the flank in a large baking dish and pour mojo to cover it.

Wrap tightly in plastic wrap and refrigerate for 1 hour or up to 8 hours. Do *not* marinate more than 8 hours, or the meat will get mushy.

Preheat outdoor grill or a ridged grill pan over medium-high heat. (You can also use a broiler.)

Brush the grates with a little oil.

Pull steak out of mojo and season both sides with salt and pepper.

Grill steak for 7–10 minutes per side, turning once, until medium-rare.

Remove steak and place on a cutting board. Let rest 5 minutes.

Thinly slice the steak across the grain.

Warm the tortillas for 30 seconds on each side in a dry skillet or on the grill, until pliable.

To make tacos, stack 2 of the warm tortillas, lay about 4 ounces of beef down the center, and sprinkle with lettuce, onion, and cheese.

Top each taco with a spoonful of Pico de Gallo salsa and garnish with lime wedges.

18. Vanilla Cider Pork with Pears

Inspired by *Cuisine*.

When the October leaves turn to their deep oranges, yellows, and reds, I yearn for this dish. It's always a favorite in my house.

Total time: 40 minutes
Serves: 4

Ingredients

3 tablespoons unsalted butter
3 Bosc pears, cored and quartered
1 pound pork tenderloin, trimmed and cut into 12 (1-inch thick) medallions
1/2 cup flour
1 cup chicken broth
1 cup cider (original recipe calls for hard cider)
1/2 cup heavy cream
1 vanilla bean, split and scraped
salt to taste
pepper to taste

Directions

Melt butter in a large skillet over medium-high heat.

Add pears and sauce until lightly browned. Remove from pan.

Season pork with salt and pepper and then dredge in flour.

Sauté medallions for 2 minutes on each side in the same pan the pears were sautéed in. Remove from pan

Combine broth, cider, and cream and then add to the pan to deglaze.

Bring to a boil and then add vanilla pod and seed. Boil until reduced by half, about 4 minutes.

Return pears and pork to the pan along with any accumulated juices. Boil until thick, about 4 minutes. Season with salt and pepper.

19. Spiedie Chicken

This recipe is the easiest that you could ever find. But don't let easy fool you. This is scrumptious and great for a crowd. Spiedie Sauce was originally made in Binghamton, New York, and can be easily bought in northeastern Pennsylvania. I would frequently make a few pounds of these in the morning before I left for work. They would be gone by the time I returned home. The boys ate them like potato chips.

Total time: 25 minutes plus marinating time
Serves: 6

Ingredients

3 pounds boneless, skinless chicken thighs
2 bottles Spiedie Sauce

Directions

Place chicken in ziplock bags and pour sauce over the chicken.

Marinate for several hours or overnight.

Heat grill to high.

Grill until thoroughly done, about 20 minutes, turning once.

This can be served hot or eaten at room temperature.

I also serve them with what I call Lilly's Dip. Lilly is a dear friend of Lebanese extraction who has been devoted to our foundation since day one. It makes a fabulous addition for this chicken.

Lilly's Dip
1 large container plain yogurt
1 English cucumber, peeled and cut into small slices
1/2–1 cup fresh mint, finely chopped
salt to taste
pepper to taste
1 tablespoon garlic powder, or to taste

Mix all ingredients together. Serve on the side with the Spiedie Chicken. It can also be served with crackers, pita, or a good piece of Lebanese bread (if you are lucky enough to find it).

20. Roast Beef Tenderloin with Horseradish Cream

Inspired by *Bon Appétit*.

I make this tenderloin each year on April 7, the anniversary of Cody's death. He loved this piece of meat and enjoyed every bite when we served it for a special dinner.

Total time: 60 minutes
Serves: 8–10

Ingredients

Horseradish Cream
1/2 cup plus 2 tablespoons sour cream
1 1/2 tablespoons (or more) drained prepared horseradish
1 1/2 tablespoons drained green peppercorns, minced or coarsely ground
kosher salt

Beef
3 cloves garlic, chopped
1 tablespoon chopped fresh thyme
2 1/2 teaspoons kosher salt

1 1/2 teaspoons pepper
1 1/2 teaspoons ground pink peppercorns
1 (3-pound) center cut beef tenderloin at room temperature
1 bunch fresh rosemary
1 tablespoon olive oil
1 tablespoon unsalted butter

Directions

For the Horseradish Cream
Whisk sour cream in a medium bowl until thickened and soft peaks start to form, 1–2 minutes.

Fold in horseradish and peppercorns; season with salt and more horseradish, if desired.

Do this ahead of time. Sauce can be made three days ahead. Cover and chill.

For the Beef
Combine first five ingredients and rub all cover meat, pressing to adhere.

Do this ahead of time. Beef can be seasoned one day ahead. Wrap in plastic and chill.

Let stand at room temperature for 1 hour before continuing.

Preheat oven to 400 degrees F.

Scatter rosemary over bottom of a large roasting pan.

Heat oil and butter in a large, heavy pan(preferably cast iron) over medium-high heat.

Sear meat until brown on all sides, about 5 minutes, and then transfer to roasting pan.

Roast meat until meat thermometer inserted into thickest part of beef registers 125 degrees for medium rare, about 30 minutes.

Transfer to a carving board. Let rest for 15 minutes.

Thinly slice tenderloin.

Serve with horseradish cream. (Meat can be served at room temperature.)

To double or triple the recipe, sear the tenderloins one at a time and then arrange crosswise in the roasting pan. (Cooking time will be the same.) Leave at least 1–2 inches between pieces of meat.

21. Chicken Marsala

Inspired by Food Network.

Total time: 30 minutes
Serves: 6–8

Ingredients

1 1/2–2 pounds chicken tenders
flour for dredging
kosher salt
pepper
1/4 cup extra-virgin olive oil
4 ounces prosciutto, thinly sliced
8 ounces cremini or porcini mushrooms,
    sliced (I have also used shitake.)
1/2 cup sweet marsala wine
1/2 cup chicken stock
2 tablespoons unsalted butter
1/4 cup chopped flat leaf parsley

Directions

Tenderize the chicken tenders until doubled in size.

Put flour in a shallow dish and season with salt and pepper.

Heat oil over medium-high heat in a large skillet.

When oil is hot, dredge both sides of chicken tenders in seasoned flour. Shake off excess.

Fry tenders in the pan until golden on each side, turning once. Do this in batches if the chicken does not fit comfortably in the pan.

Place cooked chicken to a large platter in a single layer to keep warm.

Lower the heat to medium and add prosciutto to the drippings in the pan. Sauté 1 minute.

Add the mushrooms and sauté until they are nicely browned and their moisture has evaporated, about 5 minutes. Season with salt and pepper.

Pour the marsala in the pan and boil down for a few seconds to cook off the alcohol.

Add the chicken stock and simmer for a minute to reduce sauce slightly.

Stir in the butter and return the chicken to the pan. Simmer gently for 1 minute to heat chicken through.

Season with salt and pepper and garnish with parsley.

22. Perfect Grilled Pork Tenderloin with Rosemary Orange Glaze

Inspired by *Fine Cooking*.

I really like brining, and pork tenderloin is one of my favorite meats to brine. The brine and the 7-6-5 method of grilling makes this recipe a keeper.

Ingredients

1/2 cup kosher salt
1/2 cup granulated sugar
2 (1-pound) pork tenderloins
1 recipe Rosemary Orange Glaze (recipe to follow)
ground pepper to taste
1 recipe Orange Balsamic Sauce (recipe to follow)

For the Glaze
1/4 cup frozen orange juice concentrate, thawed
2 teaspoons brown sugar
4 teaspoons minced fresh rosemary

In a small saucepan, bring the orange juice concentrate, brown sugar, and rosemary to a simmer. Simmer until the mixture reduces to about 2–4 tablespoons. Set aside to cool slightly.

For the Orange Balsamic Sauce
1 teaspoon vegetable or olive oil
3 cloves garlic, minced
1/2 teaspoons chopped fresh rosemary
1/3 cup orange marmalade
4 teaspoons balsamic vinegar

Heat the oil in a small saucepan over medium heat. Add garlic and rosemary and cook until fragrant, about 30 seconds. Stir in marmalade and vinegar. Heat until warm. After slicing the pork, add any juices from the carving board to the sauce before serving. Pass separately when serving the pork tenderloins

Directions

Brine the tenderloins: In a medium bowl, mix salt and sugar with 1 quart cool water until dissolved.

Trim the tenderloins of excess fat and silverskin, submerge them in brine, and let stand for 45 minutes.

Remove the pork from the brine, rinse thoroughly, and pat dry.

Season and grill: Rub the brined tenderloins all over with the glaze and season with salt and pepper.

Heat gas grill, turning all burners on high until the grill is fully heated, 10–15 minutes.

Put the pork on the hot grill grate. Close the lid for 7 minutes.

Turn the pork over, close the lid, and grill another 6 minutes.

Turn off the heat (keep lid closed) and continue to cook the pork for another 5 minutes.

At this point, an instant-read thermometer inserted into the middle of the thickest end of the tenderloin should read 145–150 degrees. If not, close lid and let pork continue to roast in the residual grill heat.

Remove the pork from the grill and let rest 5 minutes before carving. Cut across the grain into 1/2-inch pieces and serve immediately with sauce.

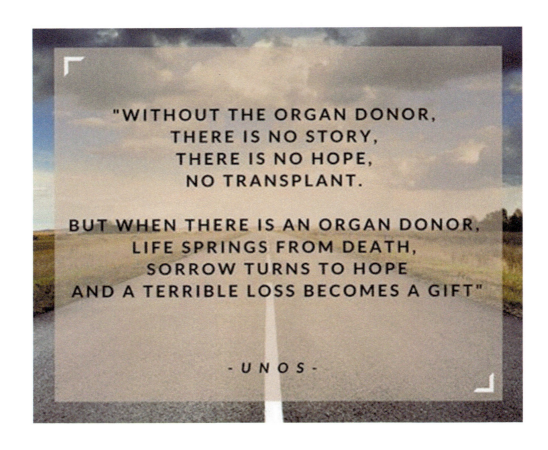

"WITHOUT THE ORGAN DONOR,
THERE IS NO STORY,
THERE IS NO HOPE,
NO TRANSPLANT.

BUT WHEN THERE IS AN ORGAN DONOR,
LIFE SPRINGS FROM DEATH,
SORROW TURNS TO HOPE
AND A TERRIBLE LOSS BECOMES A GIFT"

- U N O S -

Chapter 6:

Spuds, Sides, and Other Stuff

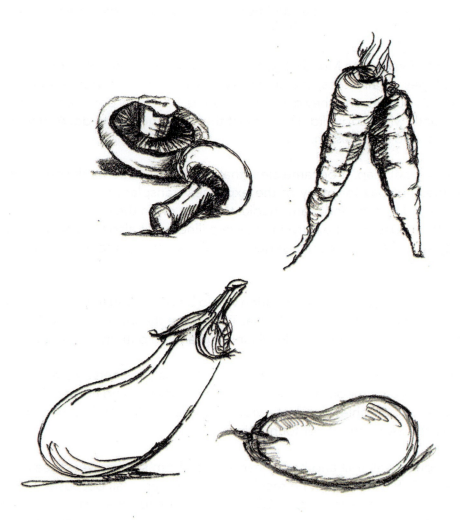

A side dish is often thought of as an unimportant element in the grand scheme of the dinner. After all, they are placed to the side.

If you really think about it, though, the correct sides don't just add to the main course; they embellish it. The side actually helps define the entire meal.

During our one hundred dinners, we have experimented with and eaten many sides. Dinner would not be the same without them.

By now, the foundation had masterfully prepared its main course: a full day to remember Cody. This day dedicated time to raise money for his scholarship fund with a three-on-three basketball tournament in the morning. The day was then completed with an evening to promote organ donor awareness.

But once again, the kids were not finished. They needed to do more. Organ donor awareness was important, but they soon realized through their work within the community that there was so much more that needed to be done.

People needed to hear Cody's story, and we needed to find a way to get those people to sign up to become donors. So then, the kids spread their wings. They ran in races, golfed in tournaments, and spoke on radio and television, all to get an important message across: the importance of becoming an organ donor.

April is Organ Donor Awareness Month. During those four weeks in 2018, the kids set up tables and booths at local colleges, retail stores, and charity events in order to attract new potential donors. They gave their time for this pursuit, and they gave of their souls. Each new donor could potentially save eight lives, and that is exactly what Cody did. That is what they all signed up to do. And that is what they tried to explain to anyone who might listen.

Then came the next giant leap. It became clear that transplant patients desperately needed financial help. Insurance does not pay for many of the expenses transplant patients and their families incur. Payment for travel, food, hotels, and many medications are often the responsibility of the patient. That patient, then, is left not just with the burden of severe illness but also the financial burden of bills they never realized they would encounter. Consequently, this can amount to a significant amount of money over time.

The kids were resolved that part of our foundation would be dedicated to easing the financial burden for transplant patients in northeastern Pennsylvania. Thus came the inception of OTAP (Organ Transplant Assistance Program). This program provides financial grants to patients awaiting transplant.

OTAP was launched on Cody's birthday, February 9, 2018. It is overseen by the young board members in the medical field, including medical residents, medical students, and nurses. They developed criteria for the grants, prepared pamphlets, and interview all of the applicants. There is a piece of our website solely dedicated to this segment of our foundation.

Our first OTAP recipient was frail and barely hanging on from severe liver disease. In April 2018, just a few months after OTAP was started, he received his new liver … all because of the selflessness of a total stranger. The financial assistance that OTAP provided made the difference of sleeping in a bed in a hotel versus in a chair in a hospital room for that patient's wife. Over the past three years, there have been many more stories from patients who received grants from OTAP—stories of hope, stories of courage, and stories of love.

This is what our foundation is about.

If our grants continue on the path they are currently on, OTAP will have given more than $100,000 to patients awaiting transplants by the time this book is published. To ease these individuals' burdens, even just slightly, continues to soothe our souls and pushes us to do more.

Cody died in Pittsburgh, three hundred miles from Scranton. The team at UPMC was nothing less than magnificent. They are what make medicine the great profession it is. Their professionalism was second to none, and their loving support at our worst moments were cherished gifts.

One of the kids suggested that we spread OTAP's wings to Pittsburgh so that people there would always remember Cody. In 2020 OTAP gave its first grant to a transplant recipient in Pittsburgh.

Now the sides of our foundation have been served and savored. By no means are these sides afterthoughts. They not only add to this beautiful entrée, called the Cody Barrasse Memorial Foundation, but they have totally embellished it.

So, spuds, sides, and other stuff, be proud. You have made the main course better than ever!

1. Boursin Mashed Potatoes

Inspired by Add a Pinch.

The Boursin cheese adds an elegant touch to mashed potatoes.

Total time: 55 minutes
Serves: 12

Ingredients

5 pounds russet or Yukon Gold potatoes, peeled and cut into chunks
1 stick butter, melted; plus 2 tablespoons cut into pieces
3/4 cup half-and-half
1 (5.2-ounce) package Boursin cheese, cut into large pieces (try garlic and fine herbs)
1 teaspoon kosher salt
1 1/2 teaspoons pepper

Directions

Place potatoes into a large saucepan and add enough water to cover, plus 1 inch. Cook over medium-low heat until fork tender, about 15–20 minutes

In a medium saucepan, melt butter and then add half-and-half. Heat until simmering.

Drain potatoes and then put them back into saucepan used to cook them.

Mash potatoes over low heat until smooth.

Add melted butter and half-and-half mixture and Boursin pieces to potatoes. Continue to mash potatoes until creamy and then mix well with a wooden spoon until light and fluffy. Stir in salt and pepper.

Pour potatoes into a serving bowl for serving.

These can be made ahead of time. Cover tightly and refrigerate until 20 minutes prior to serving. Place in preheated 350-degree oven for 20 minutes. Top with 2 tablespoons butter.

2. German Potato Salad with Dill

Inspired by *Bon Appétit*.

I usually make this for our Oktoberfest dinner. What else would I serve to remember our German brethren?

Ingredients

2 pounds small waxy potatoes, halved
1/4 cup olive oil
1/2 cup chopped onion
1/4 cup apple cider vinegar
4 scallions, sliced
4 tablespoons chopped fresh dill
1 teaspoon toasted caraway seeds
salt
pepper

Directions

Cover the potatoes with cold water. Bring to a boil and cook until tender.

Drain potatoes and transfer to a large bowl.

Meanwhile, heat 1/4 cup olive oil in a medium skillet over medium-high heat.

Add onion and season with salt and pepper.

Cook, stirring often, until soft, about 5 minutes.

Remove from the heat and mix in 1/4 cup apple cider vinegar.

Add onion mixture to potatoes, along with the scallions, dill, and caraway seeds. Toss, crushing potatoes slightly.

Season with salt and pepper to taste.

2. Loaded Slow Cooker Potatoes

Inspired from Delish.

This is a potato lover's heaven—a simple and very satisfying side.

Prep time: 15 minutes
Cook time: 5 hours
Serves: 6

Ingredients

cooking spray
2 pounds baby potatoes, halved and quartered if large
3 cups shredded cheddar cheese, divided
3 cloves garlic, minced, divided
8 slices bacon, cooked and crumbled, divided
1/4 cup sliced green onions, divided, plus more for garnish
1 tablespoon paprika, divided
kosher salt
freshly ground pepper
sour cream for drizzling

Directions

Line slow cooker with foil and spray with cooking spray. Add half the potatoes, 1 1/4 cup cheese, half the garlic, 1/3 of cooked bacon, half the green onions, and half the paprika. Season with salt and pepper.

Repeat the layers.

Cover and cook on high until potatoes are tender, 5–6 hours.

About 20 minutes before serving, top with remaining 1/2 cup of cheese and 1/3 of bacon.

Garnish with green onions.

3. Sauteed Potatoes with Chorizo

Inspired by Cooking Channel.

Total time: 35 minutes
Serves: 4–6

This is a simple recipe that works well with our May menu for Cinco de Mayo. The chorizo adds a bit of pizazz.

Ingredients

1 tablespoon vegetable oil
12 ounces pork chorizo, casings removed
1 small onion, diced
1 pound red skinned new potatoes, cut into 1/4-inch pieces and boiled
kosher salt
freshly ground pepper

Directions

Heat oil in a heavy large skillet over medium-high heat.

Add the chorizo and cook, breaking up the clumps, until dry and crisp, about 10 minutes.

Using a slotted spoon, transfer the chorizo to a paper-lined plate to absorb any additional oil.

Pour off all but 1 tablespoon of fat from the pan and heat pan over medium-high heat.

Add the onions and boiled potatoes and sauté until browned, about 12 minutes.

Stir in cooked chorizo and season with just a little salt and pepper to taste.

Serve.

4. Scalloped Corn

Inspired by *Cuisine*.

This is a very nice side that can complement most meats.

Total time: 2 1/4 hours
Serves: 12

Ingredients

Cornbread
2 cups yellow cornmeal
1 tablespoon baking powder
1/2 teaspoon kosher salt
1/2 teaspoon black pepper
1 1/2 cups buttermilk
1/4 cup vegetable oil
1 egg

Casserole
3 eggs, lightly beaten
1/2 cup half-and-half
2 tablespoons chopped fresh chives
1 teaspoon dry mustard
1/2 teaspoon kosher salt
1/2 teaspoon nutmeg
1/2 teaspoon black pepper

1 (15.25-ounce) can whole kernel corn
1 (14.75-ounce) can cream-styled corn
1/2 cup crushed saltine crackers (12 squares)

Streusel
2 tablespoons diced jarred pimentos
2 tablespoons unsalted butter
1/2 cup chopped pecans
2 tablespoons pure maple syrup

Directions

Preheat oven to 350 degrees F.

Coat an 8- x 8-inch baking pan with cooking spray.

For the Cornbread

Combine cornmeal, baking powder, salt, and pepper in a bowl.

Whisk together buttermilk, oil, and egg.

Add cornmeal mixture and whisk just until moistened but still slightly lumpy. Pour batter into prepared pan.

Bake cornbread until a toothpick inserted in the center comes out clean, about 30 minutes. Cool completely and then cut a piece and coarsely crumble 1 cup for the streusel.

For the Casserole

Preheat oven to 375 degrees F.

Coat a 2-quart baking dish with cooking spray.

Whisk together eggs, half-and-half, chives, mustard, salt, nutmeg, and pepper.

Stir in kernel corn, creamed corn, and crackers. Pour into prepared baking dish.

Bake until top is set, about 40-45 minutes.

For the Streusel

Combine 1 cup crumbled cornbread with the pimentos.

Melt butter in a skillet over medium-high heat. Add pecans and maple syrup. Bring to a boil and cook 1–2 minutes and then por over cornbread mixture, gently stirring to combine.

Season streusel with salt and sprinkle over casserole.

Bake until streusel begins to brown, about 15 minutes more

5. Sweet and Sour Red Cabbage

Inspired by *Bon Appétit*.

Here's another Oktoberfest dish!

Total time: 30 minutes
Serves: 4

Ingredients

2 tablespoons vegetable oil
1/2 onion, sliced
1/2 apple, peeled, cored, and chopped
4 cups thinly sliced red cabbage
1/4 cup apple cider vinegar
1/4 cup sugar
1/4 teaspoon celery seed
1/2 cup diced Canadian bacon

Directions

Heat oil in a heavy saucepan over medium-high heat.

Add onion and apple and sauté until golden, about 7 minutes.

Add cabbage, vinegar, sugar, and celery seed and cook until cabbage is crisp-tender and liquid is reduced to glaze, about 10 minutes.

Mix in bacon and season with salt and pepper.

6. Balsamic-Glazed Brussels Sprouts with Pancetta

Inspired by *Fine Cooking*.

Total time: 30 minutes
Serves: 2–3

Ingredients

4 ounces pancetta, diced
1–2 tablespoons extra-virgin olive oil
10 ounces brussels sprouts, trimmed
  and halved
1/4 cup balsamic vinegar
freshly ground pepper
2 tablespoons unsalted butter
kosher salt

Directions

In a heavy 10-inch straight-sided sauté pan set over medium-low heat, slowly cook the pancetta in 1 tablespoon oil until golden and crisp all over, 10–15 minutes.

With a slotted spoon, transfer the pancetta to a plate lined with paper towels, leaving the fat behind. You should have about 2 tablespoons of fat in the pan. If not, add the remaining 1 tablespoon oil.

Have 1/2 cup of water ready.

Put the pan over medium-high heat and arrange sprouts cut side down in a single layer.

Cook undisturbed until browned, 2–3 minutes.

When the sprouts are browned, add the water to the pan, cover immediately, and simmer until the sprouts are tender when poked with a fork, about 3 minutes. (If the water evaporates before the sprouts get tender, add more water, 1/4 cup at a time.)

With a slotted spoon, transfer the sprouts to a plate.

Return the pan to medium-high heat, and if any water remains, let it boil off. Add the balsamic vinegar and a few grinds of pepper.

Boil the vinegar until it is reduced to 2 tablespoons and looks lightly syrupy, about 2 minutes.

Reduce heat to low, add butter, and stir until melted. Return the sprouts and pancetta to the pan and swirl and shake the pan to evenly coat the sprouts with sauce.

Season to taste with salt and pepper.

7. Blistered Green Beans with Tomato-Almond Pesto

Inspired by *Epicurious*.

The pesto complements the green beans and makes it into an exciting dish.

Total time: 30–35 minutes
Serves: 8–10

Ingredients

2 pints cherry tomatoes
1/4 cup unsalted, roasted almonds
2 cloves garlic, minced
2 tablespoons olive oil
2 tablespoons sherry vinegar or red wine vinegar
1 teaspoon paprika
pinch cayenne pepper
kosher salt
freshly ground black pepper
3 teaspoons vegetable oil
2 pounds haricots verts (green beans), trimmed

Directions

Preheat oven to 450 degrees F.

Roast tomatoes on a rimmed baking sheet, turning once, until blistered and lightly charred, 15–20 minutes.

Let cool slightly.

Finely chop almonds in a food processor. Add garlic, olive oil, vinegar, paprika, cayenne, and half the tomatoes and pulse to a coarse pesto consistency.

Season with salt and pepper.

8. Brussel Sprouts with Maple and Cayenne

The sweetness from the maple syrup in combination with the cayenne brings out the best in these sprouts.

Inspired by Martha Stewart.

Total time: 30 minutes
Serves: 8

Ingredients

2 pounds brussels sprouts, trimmed and halved lengthwise
2 tablespoons plus 1 teaspoon extra-virgin olive oil
coarse salt
1 tablespoon pure maple syrup
1/8 teaspoons cayenne

Directions

Preheat oven to 400 degrees F.

On a rimmed baking sheet, toss sprouts with olive oil.

Roast until sprouts are browned in spots and tender when pierced with a knife, 15–20 minutes, stirring halfway through.

Meanwhile, in a small bowl, combine syrup and cayenne pepper.

Drizzle brussels sprouts with maple syrup mixture, stir to coat, and roast 1 minute.

9. Cheesy Corn Casserole

Inspired by Allrecipes.

This side has a distinctive Southern touch.

Total time: 55 minutes
Serves: 10

Ingredients

1 (11-ounce) can whole kernel corn, drained
1 (11-ounce) can creamed corn
1 (8-ounce) package sour cream
1 egg
1 (8.5- ounce) package dry cornbread mix
1 small onion, diced
1 1/2 cups shredded cheddar cheese, divided

Directions

Preheat oven to 350 degrees F. Grease a 9- x 13-inch baking dish.

In a large bowl, combine whole corn, creamed corn, sour cream, egg, dry corn bread mix, onion, and 3/4 cup of cheddar. Mix well and pour into prepared dish.

Bake in preheated oven for 25 minutes.

Remove from oven and sprinkle with remaining cheese. Bake for another 20 minutes,

10. Chili-Spiced Sweet Potato Wedges

Inspired by Food Network.

Total time: 35–40 minutes
Serves: 6

Ingredients

4 sweet potatoes
extra-virgin olive oil
salt
pepper
3 tablespoons butter, softened
1 tablespoon harissa (or other chili paste)
2 cloves garlic, minced
zest of 1 lime
chives, chopped

Directions

Preheat oven to 425 degrees F.

Cut sweet potatoes into wedges.

Toss with olive oil, salt, and pepper on a baking sheet.

Bake until browned, 20–25 minutes, flipping once.

Mix harissa, garlic, lime zest, and pinch of salt and toss potatoes in mixture. Add chopped chives and season with salt.

Serve with lime wedges.

11. Crispy Cauliflower with Capers, Raisins, and Bread Crumbs

Inspired by *Bon Appétit*.

This dish has a very interesting combination of flavors and is a great way to serve cauliflower.

Total time: 70 minutes
Serves: 4

Ingredients

1 large head cauliflower, cut into 2-inch florets
6 tablespoons extra-virgin olive oil
kosher salt
freshly ground pepper
3 cloves garlic, minced
3 tablespoons salt-packed capers, soaked, rinsed, and patted dry (I have also used bottled capers.)
3/4 cup fresh bread crumbs
1/2 cup low-sodium chicken broth
1 teaspoon anchovy paste (optional)
1/3 cup golden raisins
1 tablespoon white wine vinegar or Champagne vinegar

Directions

Preheat oven to 425 degrees F.

Toss cauliflower with 3 tablespoons olive oil in a large bowl. Season with salt and pepper.

Divide cauliflower mixture between two large, rimmed baking sheets, spreading out in a single layer.

Roast, tossing occasionally, until cauliflower is golden and crispy, about 45 minutes. *Do this ahead of time.* Cauliflower can be made 4 hours ahead. Let stand at room temperature. Reheat before using.

Meanwhile, heat remaining 3 tablespoons oil in a small saucepan over medium-low heat.

Add garlic and cook, stirring occasionally, until just golden, 5–6 minutes.

Add capers and cook until they start to pop, about 3 minutes longer.

Add bread crumbs and toss to coat.

Cook, stirring often, until bread crumbs are golden. Transfer bread crumb mixture to a plate and set aside.

Add chicken broth and anchovy paste (if using) to same saucepan. Bring to a boil.

Add golden raisins and white vinegar and cook until almost all liquid is absorbed, about 5 minutes.

Remove from heat and set aside.

Do this ahead of time. Bread crumb and raisin mixtures can be made 2 hours ahead. Rewarm raisin mixture before continuing.

Transfer warm cauliflower to a serving bowl.

Scatter raisin mixture over cauliflower and then toss to distribute evenly.

Season to taste with salt and pepper.

Sprinkle cauliflower with bread crumb mixture and parsley before serving.

12. Crispy Salt and Vinegar Potatoes

Inspired by *Bon Appétit*.

Total time: 45 minutes
Serves: 4

These potatoes are one of the kids' favorites. And for me, they bring fond memories of Cody inhaling salt and vinegar chips.

Ingredients

2 pounds baby Yukon Gold potatoes, halved (or quartered if large)
1 cup plus 2 tablespoons distilled white vinegar, divided
1 tablespoon kosher salt plus more
2 tablespoons unsalted butter
freshly ground pepper
4 tablespoons chopped fresh chives
flaky sea salt

Directions

Combine potatoes, 1 cup vinegar, and 1 tablespoon kosher salt in a medium saucepan.

Add water to cover by 1 inch. Bring to a boil, reduce heat, and simmer until potatoes are tender, 20–25 minutes. Drain and pat dry.

Heat butter in a large skillet over medium-high heat.

Add potatoes and season with kosher salt and pepper.

Cook, tossing occasionally, until golden brown and crisp, 8–10 minutes.

Drizzle with remaining 2 tablespoons vinegar.

Serve topped with chives and flaky sea salt.

13. Curry Roasted Butternut Squash and Chickpeas

Inspired by *Food and Wine*.

This has a bit of an Indian flavor and is a wonderful side for a winter meal.

Total time: 1 hour and 30 min
Serves: 12

Ingredients

2 large butternut squash, peeled, seeded, and cut into 1-inch pieces
1 (19-ounce) can chickpeas, drained, rinsed, and dried
1/4 cup extra-virgin olive oil
1 tablespoon mild curry powder
1/4 teaspoon cayenne pepper
kosher salt
freshly ground pepper
3 cups plain whole milk yogurt
3/4 cup finely chopped cilantro
4 tablespoons fresh lemon juice

Directions

Preheat oven to 375 degrees F.

In a large bowl, toss the butternut squash with the chickpeas, olive oil, curry, and cayenne. Season with salt and pepper.

Spread the squash cubes and chickpeas on a large, rimmed baking sheet and roast for 1 hour, or until tender.

Meanwhile, in a medium bowl, stir yogurt with cilantro and lemon juice. Season with salt and pepper.

Spoon the roasted butternut squash and chickpeas onto a platter and drizzle with 1/2 cup of the yogurt sauce. Serve remaining yogurt sauce on the side.

14. Green Bean and Potato Salad

Inspired by Allrecipes.

Total time: 45 minutes
Serves: 6–8

This dish is a perfect summer side. It's not too heavy and complements so many summer entrées.

Ingredients

1 1/2 pounds red potatoes
3/4 pound fresh green beans, trimmed and snapped
1/4 cup chopped fresh basil
1 small red onion, chopped
salt
pepper
1/4 cup balsamic vinegar
2 tablespoons Dijon mustard
3 tablespoons fresh lemon juice
2 cloves garlic, minced
1 dash Worcestershire sauce
1/2 cup extra-virgin olive oil

Directions

Place the potatoes in a large pot and fill with about 1 inch of water.

Bring to a boil and cook for about 15 minutes, or until potatoes are tender.

Throw in green beans to steam after the first 10 minutes. Drain and cool and then cut potatoes into quarters.

Transfer to a large bowl and toss with fresh basil, red onion, salt, and pepper. Set aside.

In a medium bowl, whisk together the balsamic vinegar, mustard, lemon juice, garlic, Worcestershire sauce, and olive oil.

Pour over the salad and stir to coat. Taste and season with additional salt and pepper if needed.

15. Green Beans and Baby Corn with Shaved Sweet Onion and Bell Peppers

Inspired by *Fine Cooking*.

This recipe is a great summer side, although it's certainly outside our comfort zone for the types of food I usually make. It uses many different spices (some I had never heard of) but is a fabulous adventure. Give it a try.

Total time: 30–35 minutes
Serves: 6–8

Ingredients

kosher salt
1 pound green beans, trimmed
3 tablespoons tamari
3 tablespoons fresh lemon juice
1 1/2 tablespoons light brown sugar
1 tablespoon peanut oil
1 teaspoon fish sauce

1 teaspoon sambal oelek
1/2 teaspoon tamarind concentrate or paste
1 (15.5-ounce) can whole baby corn, drained and rinsed
1/2 cup thinly sliced red bell pepper
1/4 cup thinly sliced sweet onion
2 tablespoons finely chopped cilantro
1/3 cup salted dry roasted peanuts, coarsely chopped

Directions

Bring a large pot of well salted water to a boil.

Blanch the beans, stirring occasionally, until crisp-tender and bright green, about 6 minutes.

Drain, rinse under cold water until cool, and transfer to a large bowl.

In a small bowl, whisk together the tamari, lemon juice, brown sugar, oil, fish sauce, sambal oelek, tamarind, and a pinch of salt.

Transfer the marinade to the beans and toss well. Let sit at room temperature for about 15 minutes, tossing occasionally.

Meanwhile, cut the corn in half lengthwise.

Add corn, pepper, and onion to the bowl with the beans and toss until well combined.

Let sit at room temperature another 10 minutes.

Season to taste with salt.

Transfer to a large serving plate and top with cilantro.

16. Green Beans with Meyer Lemon Vinaigrette and Parmesan

Inspired by *Fine Cooking*.

Vegetables in general are a difficult sell to many of the kids, but these green beans are always gobbled up quickly.

Total time: 25–30 minutes
Serves: 10–12

Ingredients

1/2 cup fresh bread crumbs
1/2 cup plus 2 tablespoons extra-virgin olive oil
kosher salt
freshly ground pepper
3/4 cup grated Parmesan cheese
finely grated zest of 1 Meyer lemon (If not available, I have used regular lemons.)
1/4 cup fresh Meyer lemon juice
1/4 cup heavy cream
2 pounds fresh green beans, trimmed

Directions

Heat oven to 350 degrees F.

In a small bowl, toss the bread crumbs with 2 tablespoons of oil., a pinch of salt, and few grinds of pepper.

Arrange in a single layer on a rimmed baking sheet and toast until golden brown, about 10 minutes. Let cool, then transfer to a bowl, and mix in the cheese.

In a medium bowl, whisk the lemon juice and zest, cream, 1/2 teaspoon salt, and 1/4 teaspoon pepper. Slowly whisk in the remaining 1/2 cup oil.

Bring a large pot of salted water to a boil over high heat.

Cook the green beans in the boiling water until tender, 4–6 minutes. Drain well.

Toss the beans with the vinaigrette. Season with additional salt and pepper if needed.

Transfer beans to a platter and sprinkle with bread crumbs.

Do this ahead of time. The crumbs can be prepared 6–8 hours prior to serving. Keep in an airtight container at room temp. The vinaigrette can be made a day ahead and stored in a covered container in the refrigerator.

17. Israeli Couscous with Mint and Lemon

Inspired by *Martha Stewart Living*.

Total time: 1 hour
Serves: 6

This is a wonderful alternative to potatoes, especially for a summer meal.

Ingredients

1 1/2 teaspoons coarse salt plus more for pasta water
8 ounces (1 1/2 cups) Israeli couscous or pearl couscous (Some do use orzo, but I prefer the couscous.)
5 tablespoons extra-virgin olive oil plus more for drizzling
1/2 cup fresh mint leaves, thinly sliced
5 scallions, thinly sliced diagonally
1/3 cup golden raisins
3 tablespoons very thinly sliced lemon zest (2–3 strips)
1/4 cup pine nuts, toasted
3 tablespoons fresh lemon juice
freshly ground pepper to taste
1/8 teaspoons red pepper flakes

Directions

Bring pot of salted water to a boil.

Add couscous and cook until al dente.

Drain and drizzle with just enough oil to coat.

Spread on a baking sheet and refrigerate 10 minutes.

Combine couscous and remaining ingredients. Let stand at room temperature for at least 30 minutes before serving

18. Maple Cinnamon Roasted Butternut Squash

Inspired by Tori Avery.

Enjoy this sweet and savory dish. Although a bit more expensive, you can find the squash already cubed in most grocery stores.

Total time: 40 minutes
Serves: 6

Ingredients

8 cups cubed butternut squash
2 tablespoons extra-virgin olive oil, divided
4 tablespoons pure maple syrup, divided
1/2 teaspoon salt, divided
1/2 teaspoon cinnamon, divided
2 pinches cayenne, divided

Directions

Preheat oven to 425 degrees F.

Line two baking sheets with foil. Spread out the cubes on the baking sheets.

Drizzle the squash on each baking sheet with 1 tablespoon oil and 1 tablespoon maple syrup.

Sprinkle each baking sheet evenly with 1/4 teaspoon salt, 1/4 teaspoon cinnamon, and a pinch of cayenne.

Toss the squash on the sheets to coat evenly.

Roast the sheets of squash for about 30 minutes, switching the baking sheets halfway through cooking.

Remove the baking sheets from the oven and turn on broiler.

Take turns placing each baking sheet under the broiler for 1–2 minutes longer to caramelize.

Serve warm.

19. Maple Ginger Roasted Vegetables

Inspired by *Food and Wine*.

Total time:1 hour, 30 minutes
Serves: 12

This is a perfect side for an autumn or winter meal—colorful, robust, and packed with flavor.

Ingredients

1 1/2 cups pecans
4 medium carrots, peeled and sliced 1/4-inch thick on the bias
2 large parsnips, peeled and sliced 1/4-inch thick on the bias
1 medium head cauliflower, cut into 1-inch florets
1 small butternut squash, cut into 1-inch pieces
1 pound brussels sprouts, halved
1/2 cup extra-virgin olive oil
1/4 teaspoon nutmeg
kosher salt
freshly ground pepper
2 tablespoons minced fresh ginger
1/2 cup pure maple syrup

Directions

Preheat oven to 425 degrees F.

Spread the pecans in pie plate and toast until fragrant, about 6 minutes. Let cool.

In a large bowl, toss the carrots, parsnips, cauliflower, squash, and brussels sprouts with olive oil and nutmeg and season generously with salt and black pepper.

Spread the vegetables on two large, rimmed baking sheets and roast for 30 minutes, until the vegetables begin to brown.

Scatter the pecans and ginger over the vegetables and drizzle with the maple syrup. Toss well.

Continue to roast the vegetables for 25 minutes longer, or until they are tender and golden.

Scrape the vegetables into a bowl and serve hot or at room temperature.

The roasted vegetables can be kept at room temperature for up to 2 hours before serving.

20. Mexican Corn Salad

Inspired by Food.

Total time: 10 minutes
Serves: 6

Ingredients

1 (16-ounce) package frozen corn, thawed
1/2 cup finely chopped fresh cilantro
1/2 cup finely chopped red onion
1/4 cup fresh lime juice
2 tablespoons minced and seeded jalapeño
1 tablespoon olive oil
1/2 teaspoon salt
1/4 teaspoon cumin
1/4 teaspoon chili powder
1/4 teaspoon black pepper
3 cloves garlic, minced

Directions

Combine all ingredients in a bowl and toss well.

Cover and chill.

Stir well before serving.

21. Old-Fashioned Scalloped Potatoes

Inspired by *Epicurious*.

There is something very special about a good old-fashioned scalloped potato. There is really no substitute.

Total time: 1 hour
Serves:6–8

Ingredients

2 cups thinly sliced onion	2 1/2 pounds boiling potatoes
9 tablespoons unsalted butter, divided	1 1/2 cups coarsely grated sharp cheddar cheese
6 tablespoons flour	1/2 cup dry bread crumbs
3 1/2 cups milk	

Directions

In a skillet, cook onion and 2 tablespoons of the butter over moderately low heat, stirring until onions are very soft.

In a heavy saucepan, melt 6 tablespoons of the remaining butter over moderately low heat, whisk in the flour, and cook the roux, whisking for 3 minutes.

Add the milk, scalded, in a stream, whisking constantly, and bring the sauce to a boil.

Simmer the sauce, whisking for 1 minute, and add salt and pepper to taste.

Peel the potatoes and slice them 1/8-inch thick.

Spread about a third of the sauce in the bottom of a well-buttered 3-quart gratin dish, at least 2 1/2 inches deep.

Cover it with a layer of potato slices, overlapping the slices slightly

Cover the potatoes with a third of the onions.

Sprinkle the onions with a third cheddar, and continue to layer the remaining sauce, potatoes, onions, and cheddar in the same manner.

Sprinkle the top with bread crumbs, dot with remaining 1 tablespoon butter cut into bits, and covered with foil. Bake the mixture in the middle of a preheated 400-degree oven for 20 minutes.

Remove the foil and bake for 30–35 minutes more, or until the top is golden and potatoes are tender.

22. Orzo with Saffron, Pine Nuts, and Currants

Inspired by *Cold Pasta* by James McNair.

This is a magnificent alternative to potatoes. It is light and filled with many intense flavors.

Total time: 30 minutes
Serves: 10–12

Ingredients

1/4 teaspoon ground saffron
1/2 cup olive oil
3 cloves garlic, minced
3 tablespoons fresh lemon juice
1/4 teaspoon cumin
2 teaspoons turmeric
1 teaspoon sugar
salt

pepper
1 pound orzo
2/3 cup pine nuts, lightly toasted
1/2 cup currants, plumped in hot water for 20
    minutes and drained
1/4 cup chopped fresh mint
1/4 cup chopped fresh parsley
3 tablespoons chopped fresh cilantro

Directions

Dissolve saffron in olive oil and let stand 15 minutes.

Add garlic, lemon juice, cumin, turmeric, sugar, salt, and pepper. Set aside.

Cook pasta in 3 quarts of boiling water until very al dente.

Drain and rinse well in cold water.

Place in a large bowl and toss with saffron-flavored oil.

Cool to room temp, occasionally stirring to coat thoroughly.

Add pine nuts, drained currants, chopped mint, parsley, and cilantro to pasta.

Serve at room temperature.

23. Roasted Balsamic Sweet Potatoes

Inspired by *Bon Appétit*.

I love roasted sweet potatoes. Add the Balsamic vinegar, and you go from a good side to a great one.

Total time: 55 minutes
Serves: 6

Ingredients

1/4 cup balsamic vinegar
1 1/2 tablespoons golden brown sugar
1/4 cup (1/2 stick) butter
1 teaspoon coarse kosher salt
3 large red-skinned sweet potatoes (yams), peeled and cut into 1 1/2-inch pieces

Directions

Preheat oven to 400 degrees F.

In a large skillet over medium heat, bring balsamic vinegar and brown sugar to boil; stir until sugar dissolves.

Reduce heat and simmer until vinegar thickens slightly, about 3 minutes.

Add butter and salt and stir until butter melts.

Add potato pieces to skillet and toss to coat.

Season potatoes with freshly ground black pepper and then spread potatoes evenly on a rimmed baking sheet.

Bake until potatoes are tender and golden, stirring occasionally, about 40 minutes.

Transfer potatoes to large platter or bowl and serve.

24. Sweet Potato Fries with Garlic and Herbs

Inspired by Williams Sonoma.

Yes, sweet potatoes can even make great fries!

Total time: 40 minutes
Serves: 4

Ingredients

2 pounds orange-fleshed sweet potatoes
2 tablespoons olive oil
1/4 teaspoon coarse sea salt plus more to taste
3 tablespoons grated Parmesan cheese
2 tablespoons chopped fresh flat leaf parsley
2 cloves garlic, minced

Directions

Preheat oven to 450 degrees F.

Cut the unpeeled potatoes lengthwise into 1/2-inch thick slices. Then cut each slice into batons about 1/4 inch wide and 3 inches long.

Place the potatoes on a baking sheet.

Drizzle with olive oil. Sprinkle with 1/4 teaspoon salt and toss to coat.

Spread the potatoes out evenly.

Roast, stirring halfway through, until potatoes are tender and browned on the edges, 20–25 minutes.

In a large bowl, stir together the cheese, parsley, and garlic.

Add the warm fries and stir gently to coat.

Season with salt and serve immediately.

25. Roasted Potato Salad with Balsamic Dressing

Inspired by Allrecipes.

For those who may not like mayonnaise-based potato salad, this fills the bill.

Total time: 1 hour
Serves: 6–8

Ingredients

10 red potatoes
3 tablespoons canola oil
1 tablespoon dried thyme
1 tablespoon chili powder
1 tablespoon kosher salt
1 tablespoon cracked black pepper
1 bunch green onions, sliced
1 cup roasted red peppers, drained and diced
1/2 cup kalamata olives, sliced
1 (10-ounce) can artichoke hearts, drained and chopped

1/4 cup chopped fresh parsley
1/2 cup crumbled Gorgonzola cheese
1/4 cup balsamic vinegar
1/4 cup extra-virgin olive oil
1 tablespoon Dijon mustard
1 teaspoon minced garlic
1 teaspoon dried oregano
1 teaspoon dried basil
salt to taste
pepper to taste

Directions

Preheat oven to 450 degrees F.

Cut the potatoes into 3/4-inch chunks and place them into a bowl.

Drizzle with canola oil and spread out onto a baking sheet. Turn potatoes so that skin sides are down.

Sprinkle the potatoes with thyme, chili powder, kosher salt, and pepper.

Bake until potatoes are golden brown, about 45 minutes.

Remove and allow to cool.

In a large salad bowl, lightly toss the cooled potatoes, green onions, roasted red peppers, olives, artichoke hearts, parsley, and Gorgonzola cheese until thoroughly combined.

Place the balsamic vinegar, extra-virgin olive oil, Dijon mustard, garlic, oregano, and basil into a blender. Pulse a few times until the dressing is thickened and creamy.

Season to taste with salt and pepper and pour over the potato salad. Toss lightly.

Chill for 4 hours before serving.

26. Patti's Almost Famous Baked Beans

Inspired by Patti Morgan.

The crowd goes crazy over these baked beans, and Patti always laughs as she brings them to dinner. Gerrity's is one of our local grocery stores. That is where the story begins, and the end result is mouthwatering.

Total time: 45 minutes
Serves: 8-10

Ingredients

3-pound container Gerrity's (deli) baked beans
2 large cans baked beans, drained
3 tablespoons ketchup
1 tablespoon yellow mustard
4 tablespoons molasses
sliced bacon to cover the top

Directions

Preheat oven to 350 degrees F.

Add all ingredients except bacon to 9- x 13-inch casserole dish. Stir well.

Top with slices of bacon to completely cover the top.

Bake at until bubbling.

If bacon is not fully cooked, place under broiler until done.

Voila!

27. Pineapple Bake

Inspired by Cathy Mineo, my friend who first planted the seed to write this book several years ago. She is a remarkably talented woman who has taken on the very important task of making sure our venue for Continue Cody's Commitment is beautiful. Each year is different, and each year, as you walk into the room, you simply cannot help but say *WOW*.

Total time: 1 hour, 15 minutes
Serves: 8–10

Ingredients

1 cup butter, softened
2 cups sugar
8 eggs
2 (20-ounce) cans crushed pineapple, drained
10 slices of bread, cubed

Directions

Preheat oven to 350 degrees F.

Cream softened butter and sugar.

Beat in eggs.

Add drained pineapple and bread cubes.

Place in baking dish and bake for 45–55 minutes, or until toasty.

28. Ripe Summer Tomato Gratin with Basil

This colorful summer dish is perfect when tomatoes are plentiful and ripe.

Inspired by MyRecipes.

Total time: 50 minutes
Serves: 8

Ingredients

2 slices whole-grain bread
6 tablespoons extra-virgin olive oil
2 tablespoons finely chopped fresh flat leaf parsley
1 teaspoon finely chopped thyme
3/8 teaspoon kosher salt, divided
3/8 teaspoon pepper, divided
1/4 cup Parmesan cheese
4 pounds sweet ripe tomatoes, mixed colors if possible
1/4 cup torn basil leaves
2 tablespoons red wine vinegar
3 cloves garlic, minced
1 large shallot, diced
2 tablespoons small basil leaves for garnish

Directions

Preheat oven to 400 degrees F.

Tear bread with your hands to form coarse crumbs and spread in an even layer on a baking sheet.

Bake for 3 minutes or until lightly toasted.

Combine bread crumbs, 2 tablespoons oil, parsley, thyme, 1/8 teaspoon salt, 1/8 teaspoon pepper, and Parmesan in a bowl.

Cut tomatoes into 1/2-inch thick slices.

Place tomatoes in a shallow dish. Sprinkle with remaining 1/4 teaspoon salt and pepper.

Add remaining 1/4 cup oil, torn basil, vinegar, garlic, and shallot. Toss gently to coat.

Arrange tomato slices in a shallow 3- or 4-quart glass or ceramic baking dish.

Pour any remaining liquid from the bowl over the tomatoes.

Bake for 15 minutes. (Tomatoes should be firm.)

Sprinkle bread crumb mixture over tomatoes and bake an additional 0 minutes or until bread crumbs are golden.

Remove dish from oven; let stand 10 minutes before serving.

Garnish with basil.

29. Roasted Broccoli with Lemon and Pine Nuts

Inspired by *Food and Wine.*

This is a very simple but tremendously tasty dish. I even eat it cold.

Total time: 40 minutes
Serves: 4

Ingredients

1 large head of broccoli, cut into florets
1/4 cup extra-virgin olive oil
kosher salt
freshly ground pepper
3 tablespoons pine nuts
2 teaspoons fresh lemon juice
1 teaspoon minced shallot

Directions

Preheat oven 400 degrees F.

On a large baking sheet, toss the broccoli florets with 2 tablespoons olive oil and season with salt and pepper.

Roast the broccoli for about 30 minutes, tossing halfway through, until browned and tender.

Meanwhile, in a small skillet, toast the pine nuts over moderate heat until light golden all over, about 4 minutes.

In a small bowl, whisk the lemon juice with the shallot and remaining 2 tablespoons of olive oil. Season the dressing with salt and pepper.

Scrape the broccoli into a serving bowl.

Add the dressing and toasted pine nuts, toss well and serve.

30. Roasted Cauliflower with Shallots and Raisins

Inspired by Martha Stewart.

The raisins sweeten up this side dish—simply delectable.

Total time: 35 minutes
Serves:4

Ingredients

1 medium head cauliflower, cut in florets
2 large shallots, thinly sliced
3 tablespoons extra-virgin olive oil, divided
coarse salt
ground pepper
2 teaspoons Dijon mustard
1 cup fresh bread crumbs
1/2 cup golden raisins

Directions

Preheat to 425 degrees F.

On a rimmed baking sheet, toss cauliflower and shallots with 2 tablespoons oil. Season with salt pepper.

Roast for 10 minutes.

Meanwhile, in a medium bowl, whisk together mustard and 1 tablespoon oil, and then stir in bread crumbs and raisins.

Sprinkle bread crumb mixture over cauliflower and roast until bread crumbs are golden brown and cauliflower is tender, about 10 minutes

31. Roasted Lemon Broccoli with Tahini Yogurt Sauce

Inspired by *Food and Wine*.

The yogurt sauce is a nice variation. I think you'll like it.

Total time: 35
Serves: 4

Ingredients

1 1/2 pounds broccoli, cut into florets
1 lemon, thinly sliced into 1/8-inch thick rounds
3 tablespoons extra-virgin olive oil
1/4 teaspoon crushed red pepper
kosher salt
1 teaspoon sesame seeds
1/2 cup plain Greek yogurt
2 tablespoons tahini
2 tablespoons fresh lemon juice

Directions

Preheat oven to 450 degrees F.

Slice florets lengthwise. Transfer to a rimmed baking sheet.

Add the sliced lemon, olive oil, and 1/4 teaspoon crushed red pepper. Season with kosher salt and toss to coat.

Roast for about 10 minutes, until lightly browned.

Stir in the sesame seeds and roast until the broccoli is tender, about 10 minutes longer.

Meanwhile, in a small bowl, whisk the yogurt with the tahini, lemon juice, and garlic. Season with kosher salt.

Spread the yogurt sauce on a platter and top with broccoli.

Garnish with sea salt and crushed red pepper.

Serve warm.

32. Roasted Peppers and Tomatoes with Herbs and Capers

Inspired by MyRecipes.

This is what summer is all about. It's a great combination of great ingredients.

Total time: 1 hour
Serves: 6–8

Ingredients

Vegetables
4 bell peppers (red, orange, and yellow)
2 pounds ripe tomatoes
2 small yellow tomatoes

Sauce
1/2 cup flat leaf parsley
12 large basil leaves
2 cloves garlic
2 tablespoons capers, rinsed

12 Nicoise olives, pitted
3 tablespoons olive oil
3/4 teaspoon sea salt
pepper to taste

Directions

Roast peppers until charred. Cool.

Wipe off blackened skin, pull out the seeds, core, and cut into strips.

Score bottom of tomatoes, blanch them, and then remove skins. Halve them crosswise, gently squeeze out the seeds, and cut into wide pieces.

Chop parsley, basil, and garlic.

Add herbs to capers, olives, oil, salt, and pepper.

Preheat oven to 400 degrees F.

Lightly oil a gratin dish.

Toss tomatoes and peppers with sauce. Cover with foil and bake 20 minutes.

Let cool before serving

33. Linda's Sautéed Vegetables

Inspired by Me.

When I realized on short notice that a large crowd was coming for a summer dinner on our deck, I cut every vegetable I had in my frig and made this. It now pops up at summer dinners all the time. And I am sure it would be enjoyed at winter dinners too!

Total time: 30 minutes
Serves: 10

Ingredients

1 zucchini, cut lengthwise and then sliced
1 yellow squash, cut lengthwise and then sliced
6 ounces shitake mushrooms
2 red peppers, sliced
2 orange or yellow peppers, sliced
1 bunch thin asparagus
3–4 ounces snow peas

2–3 cloves garlic, minced
3–4 tablespoons extra-virgin olive oil
kosher salt
pepper
3 tablespoons Italian seasoning
1 (15-ounce) can diced tomatoes
handful grated Parmesan cheese

Directions

Heat oil in large pan over medium-high heat.

Add garlic and cook until fragrant, 30 seconds

Add vegetables and sauté. Do not allow then to get too soft.

After 5–6 minutes of cooking, add diced tomatoes.

Sprinkle with Italian seasoning, salt, and pepper.

Add grated Parmesan and cook through.

Place on a serving platter. Sprinkle with another 2–3 tablespoons Parmesan. Can be eaten warm or at room temperature

34. Roasted Balsamic Green Beans

Inspired by The Rising Spoon.

This recipe takes an ordinary vegetable to an extraordinary taste.

Total time: 30 minutes
Serves: 6

Ingredients

1 pound fresh green beans
1 tablespoon sea salt
lemon pepper or black pepper to taste
granulated garlic to taste
crushed red pepper flakes to taste
2 tablespoons aged balsamic vinegar

Directions

Preheat oven to 425 degrees F.

Place the green beans in the middle of a large, rimmed baking sheet.

Pour the cooking oil over the green beans and mix them around so they are evenly coated.

Season to taste with sea salt, lemon pepper, granulated garlic, and crushed red pepper.

Spread the green beans out on the baking sheet, giving as much space between the individual beans as possible. Shake balsamic vinegar over the beans.

Bake for 10 minutes, stir the green beans, and then bake for another 5–10 minutes.

If you prefer the beans crispier, bake another 5 minutes.

35. Cheddar and Chive Mashed Potatoes

Inspired by Taste of Home.

Oh, boy … This is heaven for all you mashed potato lovers.

Total time: 1 hour, 45 minutes plus chilling time
Serves: 16

Ingredients

5 pounds Yukon Gold potatoes, peeled and cut into 1-inch pieces
1 cup butter, cubed
1 cup sour cream
2 teaspoons salt
3/4 teaspoon pepper

1/2 cup heavy whipping cream
1 1/2 cups shredded Monterey Jack cheese
1 1/2 cups shredded cheddar cheese
1/2 cup grated Parmesan cheese
2 tablespoons minced fresh chives

Toppings
1 cup shredded cheddar cheese
1 (6-ounce) can french fried onions

Directions

Place potatoes in a 6-quart stockpot and add water to cover. Bring to a boil.

Reduce heat to medium. Cook, uncovered, until tender, 10–15 minutes. Drain.

Transfer to large bowl.

Add butter, sour cream, salt, and pepper. Beat until blended.

Beat in whipping cream. Stir in cheeses and chives. Do *not* overbeat potatoes, or they will become gluey.

Transfer to a 9- x 13-inch baking dish. Cover and refrigerate overnight.

To serve, preheat oven to 350 degrees F.

Remove potatoes from refrigerator while oven heats.

Bake covered for 45 minutes, stirring after 30 minutes.

Sprinkle with toppings. Bake uncovered until heated through, about 15 minutes.

36. Roasted Carrots, Nana Style

Inspired by my mother-in-law, Nancy, better known as Nana.

Even if you don't think you like carrots, you will love these. Nana shared this recipe with me right after I was married, and I have not stopped making them. Slow roasted with some ingredients that you might never think about, they simply melt in your mouth.

Total time: 3 hours or so
Serves: 4–6

Ingredients

2 pounds carrots, peeled
1 stick of butter, melted
2 packages onion soup mix

Directions

Preheat oven to 350 degrees F.

Place carrots in a large baking dish.

Pour the melted butter over the carrots and roll the carrots in the butter until all are covered in butter.

Shake the onion soup mix over the top of the carrots.

Bake for at least 2 1/2 hours. They should be charred and soft inside.

37. Nana's Sweet Mashed Potatoes

Inspired by my mother-in-law, Nancy.

This is another great dish given to me by Nana. It's always served at Thanksgiving but also finds its way to the table many other times throughout the year.

Total time: 1 hour, 10 minutes
Serves: 6–8

Ingredients

4 sweet potatoes, peeled and cut into
   1-inch pieces
6 tablespoons butter
1 egg
6 tablespoons sugar
1 teaspoon pumpkin pie spice
pinch salt

Directions

Boil potatoes until tender, about 20 minutes.

In a mixing bowl, put potatoes with all other ingredients and beat with a handheld mixer until smooth.

Place in a 2-quart baking dish and add topping.

Topping
1 1/2 cups corn flakes, crushed (I have also used Great Grains cereal.)
1/2 cup brown sugar
1/2 cup chopped pecans
6 tablespoons melted butter

Mix all topping ingredients and sprinkle over mashed potato mixture.

Bake for 30–40 minutes.

38. Spinach with Raisins and Pine Nuts

Inspired by my Mom.

This is a go-to side. It's easy, quick, and scrumptious.

Total time: 5–10 minutes
Serves: 3–4

Ingredients

1 large container of fresh spinach
3/4 cup raisins
1/2 cup pine nuts
2 tablespoons garlic
3 tablespoons extra-virgin olive oil
kosher salt
pepper

Directions

Heat extra-virgin olive oil in a large, heavy pan.

Add spinach, raisins, and garlic. Sauté until spinach is wilted.

Add pine nuts, salt, and pepper to taste.

Serve warm.

39. Noodle Kugel

Inspired by Natalie Gelb.

This traditional dish served at a Sabbath dinner is comforting and delicious and can complement any entrée.

Total time: 1 hour
Serves: 6-8

Ingredients

16-ounce package broad noodles
1/2 pound butter, melted
1 (8-ounce) package cream cheese, softened
1 pint sour cream
5 eggs separated
1/3 cup sugar
corn flakes, crushed

Directions

Cook noodles according to package directions.

Mix together egg yolks, butter, cream cheese, sour cream, and sugar with noodles.

Sprinkle with corn flake crumbs.

Can be refrigerated overnight.

Bake uncovered for 45 minutes in a 350-degree oven.

40. Roasted Red Potatoes

This recipe has simply been around since I was born. It's on every Italian menu. It's simple. I don't know who taught it to me. But they are here to stay.

Total time: 30 minutes
Serves: 6–8

Ingredients

2 pounds baby red potatoes, cut in half
extra-virgin olive oil
kosher salt
pepper
2 tablespoons garlic, minced (or to taste)
1/2 cup grated Parmesan cheese
fresh rosemary

Directions

Preheat oven to 425 degrees F.

Place potatoes in a large bowl. Toss with all other ingredients and mix well.

Place on a baking sheet. Try not to crowd the potatoes.

Bake for 25–30 minutes or until crispy.

41. Chili Fries

Inspired by me.

These fries have a bit of a kick—just a little different than a traditional fry. And the kids love 'em hot!

Ingredients

5 pounds potatoes, sliced thin
1–2 tablespoons chili powder
kosher salt to taste
4 tablespoons canola oil

Directions

Preheat oven to 425 degrees F.

In a large bowl, whisk together oil and chili powder.

Add sliced potatoes and toss to coat evenly.

Add salt to taste and toss.

Place potatoes on a large baking sheet, keeping them in one layer.

Bake until crispy, about 25–30 minutes

Chapter 7:

Sweet Endings

Dessert is the part of the dinner that is usually sweet and served as the last course of a meal.

So why do we eat sweet things last? There are food scientists who believe that our appetites diminish after we eat too many similar foods. A sweet ending can trick our brains into wanting more food.

As we eat savory foods, our desire to eat more diminishes. Our hunger resolves. We feel full.

As we eat a meal, the joy of that first morsel of the first course vanishes. But when we eat something different, like a sweet dessert, our appetite, once again, becomes activated, and we will again be driven to continue craving food.

So, where has our journey taken us? We are a civilization of stories. Stories are what we, as humans, are all about. These past six chapters have told you our story—the story of who Cody was and how he continues to influence this world of ours through his brother and friends.

Now let us continue the story of Cody …

Once upon a time, there was a little boy. His hair was curly. His eyes were bright. He had an impish smile. He grew and he grew and became a handsome and good young man. He was gentle, yet strong. He was humble, yet courageous. Above all, he was true to himself, despite the consequences. Cody had your back. His loyalty was like no other, and he would never let you down. Cody was that guy who quietly put it all together. He was like the Pied Piper. Others followed his lead, and he was a great leader. He treated everyone the same. There was not an ounce of prejudice within him. Cody did not just believe in social justice; he lived it. He was brutally honest, both with himself and with others. He knew no other way.

And in the end, he gave himself completely through the miracle of organ donation. His loving heart went to a nine-year-old boy. That boy's mom now has the blessing to see her son ride a bike, go to school, drive a car, have a date, drink a beer … just as I did.

All because of my son …

Shortly after Cody died, a wise man told me, "You may not be ready to hear this, but I'm going to tell you anyway. Cody lived the Perfect Life. He loved and was loved. He was well educated. He was accepted to seven law schools. He never became demented. He never suffered chronic illness. And even in his death, he had no suffering. It was the Perfect Life."

For those of us left behind, the concept of the Perfect Life may be difficult to accept, but it's true. Cody completed his task here, and now he is a tremendous force on the other side.

Now we, as his family and friends, are determined to honor him by being the men and women he would want and expect us to be.

So, how about the story of the foundation?

At first glance, when you think about the journey the kids have taken, you could conceivably conclude that they did it all. They have created a well-oiled machine, but now they just have to maintain what they have achieved.

They have graduated their first Cody Barrasse Scholar from Scranton Prep. She is now about to enter her junior year in college. The other two scholars are doing well. The second is about to enter college as a freshman, and the third will be a junior at Scranton Prep. In September 2020, the fourth Cody Barrasse Scholar will begin his high school journey in Cody's name. Their lives have all been changed because of Cody and the work done by his foundation.

The kids continue to spread the word about the importance of organ donation at any opportunity they can.

OTAP continues to grow and assist those awaiting transplant with their many financial needs.

The foundation has invested what it has earned in order for the generous donations from so many loyal sponsors to continue to multiply.

All of these pieces along the journey of the foundation are similar in many ways. They are like the many courses throughout a dinner that satisfy our appetite and squelch our hunger.

Then comes the dessert, that sweet moment at the end of the meal that drives us to do more.

The dessert for us is seeing hundreds play ball for Cody. It is celebrating at a magnificent party called Continue Cody's Commitment where we promote organ donation. It is watching those financially supported by OTAP living new lives with their transplants. And, above all, it is knowing that Cody continues to live in those who study in his name and in those who lovingly house his precious organs.

So, the sweet ending is really not the end … It is actually the beginning.

And as for our foundation … to be continued.

1. Anise Wedding Cookies

Inspired by my Aunts Yolanda and Rosemarie.

Makes about 50–60 cookies

These white cookies are seen at every Italian wedding, shower, and baptism. It's just part of what happens. There are many variations of this cookie. Some are with anise, and some are without. But just know that when you see these, it's a special occasion

Ingredients

12 eggs
1 cup vegetable oil
1 cup sugar
1 small bottle of anise (vanilla can be substituted)
8 cups flour
5 heaping tablespoons baking powder

Directions

Preheat oven to 350 degrees F.

Beat eggs, oil, and sugar until bubbly and smooth. Add anise.

In another bowl, sift flour and baking powder. Add this to egg mixture a little at a time.

Work the dough with your hands. When it falls off your hands easily, it is ready to form cookies.

Roll each cookie and place on a greased cookie sheet.

Bake until bottom of the cookies are browned, about 8 minutes

Powdered Sugar Icing
Total time: 2–3 minutes
This recipe should ice 20–25 cookies.

Ingredients

2 cups powdered sugar
1 teaspoon vanilla (almond extract can also be used, depending on what you are making)
2–4 tablespoons milk

With a spoon or spatula, mix sugar and vanilla. Add milk 1 tablespoon at a time until you reach the consistency you want. It should be thick enough so that it does not run off cookies but thin enough so that the icing melts back on itself.

Apply the icing to cookies with your finger. Some chefs use a pastry bag. I find the old fashion finger to be best for me.

2. Berry Crumb Bars

Inspired by Allrecipes.

Total time: 1 hour, 20 minutes
Makes 18 bars

Ingredients

3 cups flour
1 1/2 cups sugar
2 teaspoons baking powder
1/4 teaspoon cinnamon
pinch salt
1 cup shortening
1 egg, lightly beaten
1 tablespoon cornstarch
4 cups frozen raspberries

Directions

Preheat oven to 375 degrees F. Grease a 9- x 13-inch baking pan.

Stir together flour, sugar, baking powder, cinnamon, and salt in a large bowl.

Cut in shortening with a pastry blender until mixture resembles coarse crumbs.

Stir in egg with a fork. Mixture will remain crumbly.

Press half of mixture into prepared pan.

Stir together remaining 1/2 cup sugar and cornstarch in a large bowl. Add berries and stir until coated.

Spoon fruit over crumb mixture in pan and then sprinkle with remaining half of crumb mixture.

Bake until golden and filling is bubbly, 40–45 minutes.

Let cool in pan on wire rack before serving.

3. Chocolate Pistachio Torte

Inspired by Food by Martha Stewart.

A chocolate lover's dream!

Ingredients

1 stick unsalted butter
1 cup all-purpose flour plus more for pan
1/2 teaspoon salt
1/4 teaspoon baking powder
8 ounces semisweet chocolate, coarsely chopped
1 1/4 cups sugar
1 teaspoon vanilla extract
2 large eggs
1/2 cup buttermilk
1 cup shelled, unsalted pistachios, coarsely chopped

Chocolate Ganache and Topping
1/2 cup heavy cream
4 ounces semisweet chocolate, coarsely chopped
1/4 cup pistachios, coarsely chopped

Directions

For the Cake

Preheat the oven to 350 degrees F.

Butter and flour an 8-inch round cake pan and line with parchment paper.

In a medium bowl, whisk together flour, salt, and baking powder. Set aside.

In a large heatproof bowl set over (not in) a saucepan of simmering water, melt butter and chocolate, stirring frequently, 4–5 minutes.

Remove bowl from pan.

Whisk in sugar and vanilla, followed by the eggs, buttermilk, and pistachios.

Fold in flour mixture until just combined.

Pour batter into pan. Bake until the toothpick inserted in the center comes out with a few moist crumbs attached, 60–70 minutes.

Let cake cool in the pan for 5 minutes. Run knife around edge and then invert over a wire rack. Let cool completely, about 3 hours. (To store, it can be wrapped in plastic and kept at room temperature up to three days.)

For the Ganache

In a small saucepan, bring cream to a simmer and then remove from heat.

Add chocolate and let stand for 5 minutes. Whisk until smooth. Let cool until mixture falls back in ribbons when lifted with a spoon, 2–6 minutes.

Set cake on a serving platter.

Pour ganache onto the center of cake. Using a table knife, spread evenly over the top and down the sides.

Let sit for about 30 minutes. Sprinkle top with pistachios.

4. Blueberry Sugar Cookie Pan Pie

Inspired by Heavenly Ovenz.

When the blueberries are plentiful and the summer is hot, this dessert is a great end to a meal.

Total time: 50 min
Serves: 12

Ingredients

Crust
1/2 cup butter softened
3/4 cup brown sugar
1 large egg
1 teaspoon vanilla
1 1/2 teaspoons almond extract
1–1 1/2 cups flour
1/2 teaspoon baking powder
1/4 teaspoon salt

Filling
6 cups frozen blueberries
3/4 cup brown sugar
2 tablespoons lemon juice
1/4 cup cornstarch

Directions

For the Crust
Preheat oven to 350 degrees F.

In a large bowl, beat the butter and sugar together until completely creamy.

Beat in egg, vanilla, and almond extract until smooth.

Combine flour, baking powder, and salt. Beat flour mixture into liquid until a soft dough forms.

Line 9- x 13-inch baking dish with parchment paper. Press dough into bottom and halfway up the sides of baking dish. Prick dough all over with a fork.

Bake crust for 20 minutes or until just slightly golden. Remove from oven and set aside.

For the Filling
In a large saucepan, combine the blueberries, sugar, and lemon juice. Bring to simmer over medium-high heat.

Remove some of the liquid and whisk with cornstarch in a small bowl. Stir cornstarch mixture back into blueberries and cook sauce, stirring occasionally until bubbly and thickened. Remove from the heat and pour into crust.

Bake pie for 20–25 minutes or until crust is golden brown and filling is bubbly. Remove from oven and cool completely before cutting into squares

5. Cheesecake

Inspired by my Mom.

Total time: 90 minutes
Serves: 10–12

This cheesecake was made when my Mom was making a special dinner. She served it with strawberries. The only information I have from my Mom is a list of ingredients. For the rest, I was on my own, so here it goes …

Ingredients

Crust
1 1/4 cups graham cracker crumbs
1/4 cup sugar
1/4 cup butter (may need more)

Filling
4 (8-ounce) cream cheese blocks at room temperature
1 cup sugar
6 eggs
1/2 pint sour cream

1/2 cup milk
1 teaspoon lemon juice
fresh strawberries
granulated sugar to taste

Directions

Preheat the oven to 350 degrees F.

For the Crust
Mix all ingredients together and press into bottom of a greased 9- or 10-inch springform pan.

For the Filling
Place room temperature cream cheese and sugar in a bowl.

Beat in each egg, one at a time.

Add sour cream, milk, and lemon juice and beat until smooth.

Pour filling onto crust and bake in oven for 50–55 minutes.

For Strawberry Topping
Slice fresh strawberries and add several tablespoons sugar. Let sit at room temp for an hour or so.

6. Best Chocolate Chip Cheesecake

Inspired by Delish.

This is a perfect combination of cheesecake with chocolate chips. The chocolate chip cookies bring me back to being a kid.

Prep time: 25 minutes
Total time: 8 hours
Serves: 10–12

Ingredients

Crust
1 package chocolate chip cookies
1/4 teaspoon salt
4 tablespoons unsalted butter, melted

Cheesecake
4 (8-ounce) bars cream cheese at room temperature
1 1/4 cups sugar
1 teaspoon kosher salt
1 tablespoon vanilla extract
4 large eggs, room temperature
3/4 cup sour cream
1/2 cup heavy cream
3/4 cup mini chocolate chips

Frosting
1/2 cup unsalted butter, softened
1/2 cup brown sugar
1 teaspoon vanilla
2 tablespoons pure vanilla
2 tablespoons flour
1 teaspoon kosher salt
3 tablespoons milk

Directions

Set a rack in the middle of the oven and preheat to 350 degrees F.

For the Crust
Butter a 9-inch springform pan. Wrap the bottom and sides of the pan with a double layer of aluminum foil.

In a food processor, grind cookies into fine crumbs. Add salt and pulse.

Transfer to a medium bowl and add melted butter.

Use a fork or your fingers to blend the mixture until crumbs are evenly moist.

Press mixture into the bottom and about a third of the way up the sides of the springform pan.

Transfer pan to freezer for 10 minutes.

Place pan on baking sheet and bake crust for 10 minutes and then set on rack to cool.

Reduce oven temp to 325 degrees F.

For the Cheesecake
Bring a medium saucepan or tea kettle full of water to boil.

In the bowl of a stand mixer fitted with the paddle attachment, beat cream cheese until completely smooth, about 3 minutes.

Add sugar and salt and beat until fluffy, 2 more minutes.

Add eggs, one at a time, beating after each addition.

Add sour cream, heavy cream, and vanilla. Beat for 1 more minute.

Pour a third of the cheesecake batter on top of crust and then sprinkle with a third of the chocolate chips.

Add another third of batter, followed by another third of chips.

Add the remaining batter, smooth it out, and sprinkle with the rest of the chocolate chips.

Place the cheesecake into a deep roasting pan and set it on the middle rack of the oven.

Pour enough boiling water into the roasting pan to come about halfway up the sides of the springform pan.

Bake until the top is just starting to brown and crack, about 1 hour and 30 minutes.

Turn off the oven, prop open the door, and let the cheesecake cool slowly in its water bath for 1 hour.

Remove roasting pan from the oven, carefully lift the springform pan out of the water, and remove the foil

7. Mascarpone Cannoli Cheesecake

Made by Patti Morgan.

Total time: 70 minutes to make and 5 1/2 hours inactive time
Serves: 12

Ingredients

8 large biscotti, whichever flavor is your favorite	3/4 cup sugar
4 tablespoons butter, melted	1 teaspoon vanilla
1/2 teaspoon kosher salt	1 teaspoon grated lemon zest
2 (8-ounce) bars cream cheese at room temperature	3 eggs at room temperature
1 (8-ounce) package mascarpone at room temperature	3/4 cup mini chocolate chips

Directions

Preheat oven to 350 degrees F.

Pulse the biscotti to fine crumbs in a food processor.

Drizzle in the butter, add salt, and pulse until the mixture has the texture of white sand.

Press into the bottom of a 9-inch springform pan.

Bake for 8 minutes, until the crust smells toasted and is beginning to brown.

Set aside to cool while you make the filling.

Reduce the oven temperature to 325 degrees.

In a stand mixer fitted with a paddle attachment, beat the cream cheese, mascarpone, and sugar on medium-high speed until light and fluffy, about 3 minutes, scraping down sides of bowl a few times.

Add the salt, vanilla, and lemon zest. Beat on medium speed until combined.

Add the eggs, one at a time, beating after each addition until just combined.

Scrape down the sides of the bowl and mix again.

Remove the bowl from the mixer and fold in the chocolate chips.

Pour the cream cheese mixture over the crust and spread evenly.

Bake for 45 minutes, or until the center of the cake still moves just slightly.

Allow the cheesecake to cool on a wire rack for 1 hour.

Cover with plastic wrap and refrigerate for at least 4 hours or overnight.

Run a knife around the edge of the pan before releasing the collar.

8. Apple Cake

Inspired by my Mom.

This cake is one of my favorite fall desserts. It's great for breakfast too!

Total time: 1 hour, 45 minutes
Serves: 10–12

Ingredients

5 tablespoons sugar
2 teaspoons cinnamon
6–8 apples (I use Granny Smith), peeled and sliced
2 cups sugar
1 cup oil
4 eggs
3 cups flour
1 tablespoon baking powder
1/4 cup orange juice
2 1/2 teaspoons vanilla

Directions

Preheat oven to 350 degrees F.

Sprinkle apples with cinnamon and 2 teaspoons sugar. Set aside.

Mix sugar and oil.

Add eggs, one at a time, until creamy.

Add flour and baking powder, alternating with orange juice and vanilla.

Pour some batter on the bottom of a greased 9-inch tube pan.

Then add apples and top with the rest of the batter.

Bake for 1 1/2 hours.

9. Blueberry Cake

Inspired by my childhood girlfriend Sharon, who always made me smile. She too left us much too soon. I bake this in her honor.

Total time: 1 hour, 15 minutes
Serves: 10–12

Ingredients

3/4 cup shortening
1 1/4 cups sugar
4 eggs
1 teaspoon vanilla
3/4 cup orange juice
3 cups flour
1 tablespoon baking powder
1 teaspoon salt
1 quart blueberries

Directions

Preheat oven to 350 degrees F.

Cream shortening, sugar, and eggs.

Add vanilla and orange juice and mix.

Add flour, baking powder, and salt. Beat well.

Fold in the blueberries.

Bake in a tube pan for 1 hour.

10. Chocolate Almond Cake with Sugared Cranberries

Inspired by Food Network.

This cake is a bit time-consuming and not a slam-dunk dessert. But it is worth every bit of the effort. It's the type of dessert that makes you say, "It was definitely worth the calories"!

Prep time 1 hour
Inactive time: 2 hours, 25 minutes
Cook time: 35 minutes
Serves: 10–12

Ingredients

Sugared Cranberries
1 1/2 cups granulated sugar, divided
2 cups cranberries
1/2 teaspoon ground cardamon

Cake

nonstick cooking spray
2 cups all-purpose flour
1/2 cup almond flour
1 1/2 teaspoons baking powder
1 teaspoon baking soda
1/2 teaspoon salt
1/2 teaspoon ground allspice
1/2 teaspoon ground cardamom

3/4 cup unsweetened processed Dutch cocoa powder
1 cup water
3 large eggs
2 cups granulated sugar
1 cup butter milk
1/2 cup vegetable oil
3 teaspoons vanilla extract

Frosting

4 sticks unsalted butter at room temperature
6 cups powdered sugar
1 teaspoon salt
1 tablespoon vanilla
1 teaspoon almond extract
2 tablespoons milk
2 tablespoons almond flavored liquor (or use more milk)

Directions

For the Sugared Cranberries
Bring 3/4 cup sugar and 3/4 cup water to simmer in a medium saucepan.

Cook, stirring until the sugar dissolves, about 2 minutes.

Put the cranberries in a large bowl and pour the syrup over them. Let sit for 1 hour.

Whisk the remaining 3/4 cup sugar with cardamon in a large bowl.

Drain the cranberries, add to spiced sugar, and toss to coat.

Spread the cranberries and sugar on a rimmed baking sheet.

Let sit, rerolling the cranberries in sugar occasionally. Let sit until dry, about 2–3 hours.

For the Cake
Preheat oven to 325 degrees F.

Coat two 9-inch round cake pans with cooking spray and line the bottoms with parchment paper. Coat the paper with cooking spray.

Whisk the two types of flour, baking powder, baking soda, salt, allspice, and cardamon in a large bowl. Set aside

Put the cocoa powder in a separate large bowl.

Heat water in a small saucepan until almost simmering. Pour over the cocoa powder and whisk until smooth. Set aside until slightly cooled, about 10 minutes.

Add the eggs to the cocoa mixture and beat with a mixer on medium-high speed until just combined.

Add sugar, buttermilk, vegetable oil, and vanilla. Beat until combined.

Reduce the mixer speed to low and gradually add the flour mixture.

Increase the speed to medium and beat until smooth, about 1 minute.

Divide the batter evenly between the two pans. Lightly tap each pan on the counter to get rid of the air bubbles.

Bake until toothpick inserted in the center comes out clean, about 30–35 minutes.

Transfer to rack and let cool 10 minutes in the pans and then invert the cakes onto the rack to cool completely. (The layers can be made a day ahead. Let cool and wrap tightly.)

For the Frosting
Beat the butter, powdered sugar, and salt in a large bowl with mixer on medium speed until just combined.

Add vanilla and almond extract. Increase speed to high and beat until creamy, about 3 minutes.

Add milk and almond liqueur. Beat until light and fluffy, 1–2 more minutes.

Halve 1/2 cup of the sugared cranberries.

Place one cake layer on a plate or cake stand.

Spread with 1 cup frosting and then sprinkle with the halved cranberries.

Top with the second cake layer. Cover the top and sides of the cake with the remaining frosting.

Top with the remaining sugared cranberries.

Tada!

11. Coffee Cake

Inspired by my Mom.

Total time: 1 hour, 15 minutes
Serves: 8–10

This is another one of my Mom's favorites. If we got unexpected company, she would whip this one up quickly. Most of the ingredients are in your pantry. It is great with a scoop of vanilla ice cream. It is a cake lover's dream for breakfast.

Ingredients

1 stick butter
2 cups flour
1 cup sugar
2 eggs
1 cup sour cream

1 teaspoon baking powder
1 teaspoon baking soda
1/2 cup ground nuts
2 tablespoons sugar
1 teaspoon cinnamon

Directions

Preheat oven to 350 degrees F.

Cream sugar and butter.

Then add sour cream

Sift dry ingredients and add gradually.

Lastly, add eggs. Blend well.

Mix together nuts, sugar, and cinnamon

Grease tube pan.

Put 1/2 the batter into pan and sprinkle half of the nut mixture over the batter.

Pour the rest of better into pan and sprinkle with remaining nuts.

Bake for 50–55 minutes.

12. No-Bake Orange Creamsicle Cheesecake

Inspired by Patti Morgan.

It *really* does taste like a Creamsicle!

Total time: 20 minutes
Serves: 8–10

Ingredients

12 ounces vanilla wafers
1 1/2 cups sugar, divided
1/2 stick unsalted butter, melted
2 (8-ounce) packages cream cheese at room temperature
2 cups heavy cream
1 (3-ounce) box orange gelatin
1 cup boiling water
1/2 cup powdered sugar
1/2 teaspoon vanilla
zest of 1 orange

Directions

Pulse vanilla wafers in a food processor until it resembles crumbs.

Add 1/2 cup sugar and melted butter, pulsing to combine

Spray a 9-inch springform with cooking spray and press mixture into bottom of the pan and slightly up the sides. Chill in the freezer for at least 30 minutes.

In a large mixing bowl, beat together cream cheese and 1 cup sugar with a handheld mixer until smooth and creamy. Set aside.

In a separate bowl, whisk together orange gelatin and boiling water until dissolved and set aside.

In a separate medium bowl, whip heavy cream, vanilla, and powdered sugar until stiff peaks form.

Combine half of the whipped cream mixture with the orange gelatin mixture and the other half with the cream cheese mixture.

Alternate spreading each mixture into the pan, starting with the cream cheese mixture and ending with whipped cream. Chill for at least 4 hours or overnight.

13. Blackberry Slump

Inspired by *Epicurious.*

The first time I made this was simply because I never heard of a slump. I still get cobblers, crisps, buckles, and slumps all mixed up. But this particular recipe has become one of my favorite fruit desserts. When I do not have enough blackberries, I add strawberries and blueberries. Add that wonderful scoop of vanilla ice cream. What a fabulous way to end a meal.

Total time: 1 hour
Serves: 4–6

Ingredients

4 cups fresh blackberries
1 cup sugar, divided
1 cup flour
1 1/2 teaspoons baking powder

1/2 teaspoon salt
3/4 cup milk
2 tablespoons unsalted butter, melted

Directions

Preheat oven to 375 degrees F.

Put berries in ungreased 5- or 6-cup gratin dish or deep-dish pie plate and sprinkle with 3/4 cup sugar.

Sift flour, baking powder, salt, and remaining 1/4 cup sugar into a bowl.

Add milk and butter and whisk until smooth. Pour over the berries. (Don't worry if the berries are not completely covered.)

Bake slump in middle of oven until golden, 40–45 minutes. Serve warm.

This can easily be doubled if you have a baking dish big enough.

14. Cherry Garcia Brownies

Inspired by Delish.

Brownies are magnificent on their own, but add some cherries, and these will simply knock you out.

Total time: 1 hour
Serves: 12

Ingredients

butter and flour for greasing pan
1 box brownie mix plus ingredients called for on box (I use fudgy brownies.)
1 (8-ounce) package cream cheese, softened
1 teaspoon vanilla extract
1 large egg
1/2 cup sugar
1 cup cherries, pitted and quartered (I have used frozen ones in a pinch.)
1/2 cup chocolate chips

Directions

Preheat oven to 350 degrees F.

Grease 8- x 8-inch baking dish with butter and sprinkle with flour.

Prepare brownie batter according to package instructions.

In a medium bowl, beat cream cheese, vanilla, egg, and sugar with an electric mixer until light and fluffy.

Stir cherries and chocolate chips into cream cheese mixture.

Pour brownie batter into prepared baking dish. Dollop the cherry cream cheese mixture over the brownie layer.

Run a knife through mixture and batter to create a swirled effect.

Bake until a toothpick inserted into the middle of the brownie comes out mostly clean, about 45 minutes. Cool in pan completely and then slice into small squares.

15. Chewy Peanut Butter Chocolate Chip Cookies

Inspired by Allrecipes.

All I can say is *wow*.

Total Time: 30 minutes
Makes: 28 cookies

Ingredients

2 1/2 cups flour
1 teaspoon baking soda
1/2 teaspoon salt
1/2 cup butter, softened
1/2 cup peanut butter
1 cup packed brown sugar
1/2 cup white sugar
2 eggs
2 tablespoons light corn syrup
2 teaspoons water
2 teaspoons vanilla extract
2 1/2 cups chopped semisweet
   chocolate (I use chocolate chips.)

Directions

Preheat oven to 375 degrees F.

Stir together flour, baking soda, and salt in a bowl.

In a large bowl, beat together butter and peanut butter with an electric mixer for 30 seconds.

Add brown and white sugars and beat until smooth.

Beat in eggs, one at a time.

Add corn syrup, water, and vanilla and mix well.

Beat in flour mixture and then fold in chocolate pieces.

Drop by 3-tablespoons portions 3 inches apart onto ungreased baking sheets.

Bake until edges are golden, 11–12 minutes. Let cool 2 minutes and transfer to wire racks to cool completely.

16. Chocolate Chip Bread Pudding with Cinnamon Rum Sauce

Inspired by *Bon Appétit.*

I love bread pudding. It started as a dessert made by peasants with the simplest of ingredients, sugar, eggs, cream, and bread, but there is nothing peasant like about this dessert.

Total time: 1 hour, 45 minutes
Serves: 8–10

Ingredients

Pudding
1 (1-pound) loaf brioche or egg bread cut into 1-inch cubes (I use the cinnamon raisin loaf from Panera.)
10 tablespoons unsalted butter, melted, divided
1 cup semisweet chocolate chips
2 1/2 cups half-and-half (I have also used heavy cream.)
1 cup sugar
6 large eggs
4 large egg yolks
2 tablespoons vanilla
1/4 teaspoon salt
2 tablespoons brown sugar
Cinnamon Rum Sauce (recipe to follow)

Directions

Preheat oven to 350 degrees F.

Butter 9- x 13-inch baking dish.

Place bread cubes in a large bowl. Pour 8 tablespoons melted butter over bread and toss to coat.

Add chocolate chips and toss to combine. Transfer mixture to prepared dish.

Whisk half-and-half, sugar, eggs, egg yolks, vanilla, and salt in a large bowl to blend.

Pour over bread cubes in dish. Let stand 30 minutes, occasionally pressing bread cubes into custard. (It can be prepared 1 day ahead up to this point. Cover and refrigerate.)

Drizzle remaining 2 tablespoons melted butter over pudding and sprinkle with brown sugar.

Bake bread pudding until puffed, brown,and set in center, about 1 hour. Serve warm with Cinnamon Rum Sauce.

17. Cinnamon Rum Sauce

Makes about 1 1/2 cups

Ingredients

2 sticks unsalted butter
1 cup packed dark brown sugar
1 teaspoon cinnamon
1/2 teaspoon salt
1/4 cup dark rum
1 tablespoon vanilla

Directions

Melt butter in a heavy saucepan over medium-high heat.

Add brown sugar, cinnamon, and salt and whisk until sugar is dissolved and mixture is bubbling and smooth, about 6 minutes.

Remove from heat. Whisk in dark rum and vanilla.

Serve warm.

18. Chocolate Pepper Cookies

Inspired by my Aunts Rosemarie and Yolanda.

Another Italian favorite at showers, weddings, baptisms, or any other occasion worth celebrating. There are multiple variations of this cookie. This is my Aunts' version. For any special event, we all get together and make them. It can be messy and loud, but that's part of how they operate. One thing can be guaranteed: It is always fun. This particular version does not actually use pepper. Cloves are the magic ingredient.

Total time: 1 1/2 hours
Makes about 70 cookies

Ingredients

1 1/2 cups vegetable oil
8 cups flour
1 3/4 cups sugar
1 cup cocoa
4 tablespoons baking powder

4 tablespoons ground cloves
1 tablespoon cinnamon
1 bag semisweet chocolate chips
2 cups chopped nuts
1 box raisins

Directions

Preheat oven to 350 degrees F.

Soak raisins in 2 cups of very hot but not boiling water. Set aside.

Mix all dry ingredients.

Add oil and work with your hands.

Add water and raisins and continue to mix.

Add chips and nuts and mix until combined.

Bake until firm, about 10–12 minutes

Let cool completely. Frost with simple white frosting.

19. Cream Puff Cake

Inspired by Cody's Aunt Janine.

Ingredients

1 stick unsalted butter
1 cup water
1 cup flour
4 eggs
2 (3.4-ounce) packages vanilla instant pudding
8 ounces cream cheese
4 cups milk
1 (8-ounce) tub of frozen whipped topping
chocolate syrup

Directions

Preheat oven to 350 degrees F.

Grease a 9- x 13-inch baking sheet.

Put butter and water in a small saucepan and bring to a boil.

Lower heat and add the flour. Mix vigorously with a wooden spoon until blended.

Remove from heat, add the eggs, and mix until thickened. It will be sticky.

Using a spatula, spread mixture evenly on the baking sheet.

Bake for 30 minutes. Take out of oven and place a clean kitchen towel over the crust, pressing down gently to remove the bubbles. Let cool.

In the meantime, make the pudding according to package instructions.

Beat cream cheese into pudding.

Once crust is cooled, layer the pudding mix and whipped topping on top.

Drizzle with chocolate syrup.

20. Creamy Caramel Flan

Inspired by Taste of Home.

The combination of custard and caramel is spectacular. Perfect for Cinco de Mayo.

Total time: 75 minutes
Serves: 8–10

Ingredients

3/4 cup sugar
1 (8-ounce) package cream cheese
5 large eggs
1 (14-ounce) can sweetened condensed milk
1 (9- or 12-ounce) can evaporated milk
2 teaspoons vanilla

Directions

In a heavy saucepan, cook and stir sugar and water over medium-low heat until melted and golden, about 15 minutes. Brush down crystals on the side of the pan with additional water if necessary.

Quickly pour into a round ungreased 2-quart baking or souffle dish, tilting to coat the bottom. Let stand for 10 minutes.

Preheat oven to 350 degrees F.

In a bowl, beat the cream cheese until smooth.

Beat in eggs, one at a time, until combined.

Add remaining ingredients and mix well.

Pour mixture over caramelized sugar.

Place the dish into a larger baking pan. Pour boiling water into larger pan to a depth of 1 inch.

Bake until the center is just set (mixture will jiggle), 50–60 minutes.

Remove dish from the larger pan to a wire rack and cool for 1 hour.

Refrigerate overnight.

To unmold, run knife around edges and invert onto a large, rimmed serving platter

21. Crockpot Apple Caramel Crumble

Inspired by Nancy Patterson, my friend from the hospital.

Serves: 8

Ingredients

1 cup brown sugar
1/2 cup granulated sugar
6 large apples, peeled and cut into chunks
1/4 teaspoon salt
1 teaspoon cinnamon

Directions

Mix sugars and spread evenly on bottom of crock pot.

Toss apples with salt and cinnamon

Layer over sugars in crock pot.

For the Topping
2/3 cup oats
2/3 cup brown sugar
1/4 cup flour
1/2 teaspoon salt
3–4 tablespoons butter, softened
1 teaspoon vanilla

Mix all ingredients in a bowl.

Use fingers to distribute evenly over apples.

Cook on low for 4 hours or on high for 2 hours.

Let sit on off for 1 hour.

Serve with vanilla ice cream

22. Dirt

Inspired by many mothers at Nativity Grade School.

This dish is the most infamous at our dinners. It was Cody's favorite dessert, one that was a treat from the time he was a little boy. This is the *only* recipe the kids ask me to make each month. I have made this for one hundred dinners with joy in my heart, remembering when these kids were really kids. I could not imagine dinners without it.

Total time: 20 minutes
Serves: 10

Ingredients

1 bag of chocolate sandwich cookies
1 cup powdered sugar
1/4 cup butter
1 (8-ounce) package cream cheese
2 (3-ounce) packages instant vanilla pudding
4 cups milk plus 1/2 cup
1 (12-ounce) container frozen whipped topping

Directions

Make vanilla pudding according to package instructions.

Cream together butter, cream cheese, and powdered sugar.

Add vanilla pudding, 1/2 cup milk, and whipped topping.

Crush cookies in a food processor. Fold two-thirds of the crumbs into the pudding mixture.

Place in trifle bowl. Top with remaining third of cookie crumbs.

Some purists feel that gummy worms should be put in the dirt … Our kids prefer the wormless version.

23. Fresh Cherry Galette

Inspired by *Cooking Light*.

Total time: 1 hour, 11 minutes
Serves: 6

Cherries are such a part of summer. This cherry dessert is not too sweet and packs a powerful punch.

Ingredients

1/2 (14.1-ounce) package refrigerated pie crust
3 tablespoons sugar, divided
1 1/2 teaspoons cornstarch
4 cups pitted Rainier cherries (I have used other types of cherries.)
1/2 teaspoon grated lemon rind
2 teaspoons fresh lemon juice
1 1/2 teaspoons buttermilk
1 tablespoon turbinado sugar

Directions

Preheat oven to 400 degrees F.

Line a baking sheet with parchment paper. Unroll pie dough onto parchment, and roll out a 12 1/2-inch circle.

Combine 1 tablespoon sugar and 1 1/2 teaspoons cornstarch, stirring with a whisk.

Sprinkle cornstarch mixture over dough, leaving a 2-inch border.

Combine the cherries, remaining 2 tablespoons granulated sugar, rind, and juice. Toss well to coat.

Arrange cherry mixture over dough, leaving a 2-inch border.

Fold dough border over cherries, pressing gently to seal. (Dough will only partially cover cherries.)

Brush edges of dough with buttermilk.

Sprinkle turbinado sugar over cherries and edges of dough.

Bake for 25 minutes or until dough is browned and juices are bubbling.

Remove from oven and cool in pan at least 20 minutes before serving.

24. Homemade Gingersnaps

Inspired by Laurie Quinn.

Total time:30 minutes
Makes: 5 dozen

Ingredients

2 cups flour	3/4 cup shortening
1 tablespoon ground ginger	1 cup white sugar
2 teaspoons baking soda	1 egg
1 teaspoon cinnamon	1/4 cup dark molasses
1/2 teaspoon salt	1/3 cup cinnamon sugar

Directions

Preheat oven to 350 degrees F.

Mix flour, ginger, baking soda, cinnamon, and salt in a mixing bowl.

Place shortening in another mixing bowl and beat until creamy.

Gradually beat in sugar, then egg, and then molasses.

Blend the dry ingredients slowly into mixing bowl No. 1, and mix until soft dough forms.

Roll into 1-inch balls and roll in cinnamon sugar.

Bake on ungreased sheet for 10 minutes.

Gingersnap Dip
Total time: 20 minutes
Makes: 3 cups

Ingredients

1 (8-ounce) package cream cheese
1 cup powdered sugar
2 teaspoons pumpkin pie spice
8 ounces frozen whipped topping

Mix all ingredients together.

Dip cookies and enjoy.

25. Hello Dollies

Inspired by Cody's Aunt Janine.

Total time: 45 minutes
Makes: 2 dozen bars

Ingredients

cooking spray
1 1/2 cups graham cracker crumbs
1/2 cup butter, melted
1 (14-ounce) can sweetened condensed milk
2 cups (12-ounce package) semisweet chocolate chips
1 1/3 cup flaked coconut
1 cup chopped walnuts

Directions

Preheat oven to 350 degrees F.

Coat 9- x 13-inch baking dish with spray.

Combine graham cracker crumbs and butter in a small bowl. Press into bottom of prepared pan.

Pour condensed milk evenly over crumb mixture.

Layer evenly with chocolate chips, coconut, and nuts. Press down firmly with fork.

Bake for 30 minutes.

26. Aggie's Famous Peanut Butter Brownies

Inspired by our next-door neighbor, Aggie Holland. She was like another mom to my boys. Aggie; her husband, Tim; and their three kids are simply family.

This is one of the kids' absolute favorites!

Total time: 1 hour
Serves: 12

Ingredients

Brownies
any brand of brownie mix (Aggie uses dark chocolate.)
1 extra egg

Icing
1 (16.3-ounce) jar peanut butter (Aggie uses crunchy.)
1 cup powdered sugar
2 teaspoons vanilla
1/4 cup milk

Prepare the brownies as directed on the package, but use the additional egg to make them more cakelike in consistency.

Combine all the ingredients for the icing with hand mixer, adding small amounts of milk to reach desired consistency.

Spread icing on top of cooled brownies.

27. Peach Pie Crumble Bars

Inspired by Martha Stewart.

This is a great dessert to use when you have leftover peaches. I have also used frozen peaches without a problem.

Prep time: 30 minutes
Total time: 3 hours
Makes 16 bars

Ingredients

Crust
1 stick plus 5 tablespoons unsalted butter at room temperature
1 cup sugar
2 cups flour
2 teaspoons coarse salt

Filling
3 1/2 cups diced peaches
1/2 cup sugar
2 tablespoons flour
1 tablespoon fresh lemon juice
1/2 teaspoon coarse salt

Directions

Preheat oven to 375 degrees F.

Butter an 8- x 8-inch cake pan and line with parchment, leaving a 2-inch overhang on 2 sides. Butter the parchment paper.

For the Crust
Beat butter with sugar in a bowl until light and fluffy, about 3 minutes. Scrape down bowl.

Add flour and salt. Beat until dough forms clumps but does not completely hold together.

Press 2 1/2 cups flour mixture into bottom and 1 inch up sides of prepared pans.

For the Filling
Stir together peaches, sugar, flour, lemon juice, and salt in a bowl.

Pour fruit mixture into crust.

Crumble remaining flour mixture evenly over top, squeezing to create clumps.

Bake until bubbling in center and crust is golden about 1 hour and 10 minutes. (If browning too quickly, tent top with foil.)

Let cool 20 minutes.

Remove from pan and let cool completely on a wire rack, about 1 hour.

Cut into 2-inch squares.

28. Pizzelles

Inspired by me.

What is a pizzelle, anyway? It's a true Italian delicacy that looks like a big wafer. It should be thin and crisp but not hard like a rock. Traditionally, they are laced with anise. Pizzelles were one of the ways my family prepared for Christmas. We actually had a pizzelle night. The house was filled with friends and family. The kids helped, and we all made a mess of the kitchen. The end result was a night filled with lots of love and laughter and several hundred beautiful cookies. One was always put out for Santa along with potato chips and Diet Coke. After all, Santa gets sick of only having cookies and milk.

Total time: 90 minutes
Makes 60 or so

Ingredients

6 eggs
1 cup butter, melted
1 1/2 cups of sugar
2 1/2 cups flour
2 tablespoons anise (or vanilla)
4 teaspoons baking powder
1 cup finely chopped walnuts

Directions

Beat eggs and add sugar gradually, continuing to beat until smooth.

Add cooled butter and anise to the above egg mixture.

Then add flour and baking powder .

Blend into eggs until smooth.

Heat pizzelle iron until very hot. Coat iron with cooking spray

Place a heaping teaspoon of batter onto each side of iron.

Close lid and cook until golden. This may take some practice, as each iron cooks differently.

Place finished cookies on a counter covered with wax paper.

When cool, sprinkle with powder sugar.

29. Plum Kuchen

A sweet plum is a real treat. Putting them in a great dessert is a delicacy.

Total time: 1 hour, 10 minutes
Serves: 8–10

Ingredients

1 1/2 cups flour
2/3 cup plus 2 tablespoons sugar, divided
2 tablespoons brown sugar
1 teaspoon baking powder
3/8 teaspoon salt, divided
1/8 teaspoon cardamom
7 tablespoons butter, cubed and divided

1/2 cup milk
1 teaspoon vanilla
1 large egg
cooking spray
1 1/2 pounds plums, quartered and pitted
1 teaspoon grated lemon rind
1/4 teaspoons allspice

Directions

Preheat oven to 425 degrees F.

Combine flour, 2 tablespoons granulated sugar, baking powder, 1/4 teaspoon salt, and cardamom in a medium bowl, stirring well with a whisk.

Cut in 4 tablespoons butter with a pastry blender or 2 knives until mixture resembles coarse meal.

Combine milk, vanilla, and egg in a bowl, stirring with a whisk.

Add milk mixture to flour mixture and stir until combined.

Spoon batter into a 9-inch round metal cake pan coated with cooking spray.

Arrange plums in a circular pattern over batter.

Combine remaining 2/3 cup granulated sugar, 1/8 teaspoons salt, lemon rind, and allspice in a small bowl, stirring well.

Place remaining 3 tablespoons butter in a bowl and microwave on high 30 seconds or until butter melts. Stir into sugar mixture.

Sprinkle plums evenly with sugar mixture.

Bake for 35 minutes or until browned and bubbling.

Cool in pan on a wire rack for 1 hour

30. Pumpkin Cheesecake with Bourbon Spiked Cream

Inspired by Emeril Lagasse and Food Network.

This one is a tradition at Thanksgiving. Gobble, gobble, gobble …

Total time: 1 hour, 55 minutes
Serves: 12

Ingredients

Cheesecake
1 1/2 cups vanilla wafer crumbs (about 45 crushed wafers)
1 cup ground pecans
1 stick unsalted butter, melted
4 (8-ounce) packages cream cheese, cubed and softened
1 cup packed light brown sugar
6 large eggs
1/2 cup heavy cream
1/2 cup flour
pinch of salt
1/2 teaspoon cinnamon
2 teaspoons vanilla
2 cups canned pumpkin

Topping
2 cups sweetened whipped cream
dash bourbon
1/4 cup half-and-half
1 tablespoon unsalted butter
8 ounces semisweet chocolate chips
1/4 teaspoon vanilla

Directions

For the Cheesecake
Preheat oven to 350 degrees F.

Combine the wafer crumbs, ground pecans, and melted butter in a bowl. Press into bottom of a 12-inch springform pan.

In a food processor fitted with metal blades, mix the cream cheese until smooth.

Add the brown sugar and process until blended.

Add eggs, one at a time, processing until fully incorporated. Next, blend in heavy cream.

Add the flour, salt, cinnamon, and vanilla and blend until smooth.

Add pumpkin and blend until smooth.

Pour the filling over the crust in the pan.

Bake 1 hour and 15 minutes, or until cheesecake is just set.

Remove from oven. Use a knife to loosen cake from the sides of the pan. This will prevent it from splitting down the center. Let it cool completely before slicing.

For the Topping
Combine the whipped cream and bourbon in a bowl and mix until blended.

For the chocolate sauce, combine the half-and-half and butter in a small heavy-bottomed saucepan over medium heat. Heat until a thin, paperlike skin appears on top. *Do not boil.*

Add the chocolate chips and vanilla and stir until the chocolate melts and the mixture is smooth. Remove from heat and let cool.

Remove the side of the springform pan and slice the cake. Top each piece with a drizzle of chocolate sauce and some bourbon whipped cream.

31. Pumpkin Roll

Inspired by Aunt Janine.

Ingredients

3 eggs
1 cup sugar
2/3 cup canned pumpkin
1 teaspoon lemon juice
3/4 cup flour
1 teaspoon baking powder
2 teaspoons cinnamon

1 teaspoon pumpkin pie spice
1 cup chopped walnuts
1/2 cup powdered sugar
1 (8-ounce) package cream cheese
4 tablespoons butter, softened
1/2 teaspoon vanilla

Directions

Preheat oven to 375 degrees F.

Beat eggs until fluffy.

Add sugar and beat until blended.

Stir in pumpkin, lemon juice, flour, baking powder, cinnamon, and pumpkin pie spice.

Grease and flour a 9- x 13-inch baking sheet.

Spread mixture on baking sheet and sprinkle with chopped nuts.

Bake for 15 minutes.

In the meantime, lay out a clean kitchen towel and sprinkle it with powdered sugar.

When the cake is done, take it out of the oven and gently flip it over on the towel.

Roll it up and let it cool. While it is cooling, make the filling.

Beat powdered sugar, cream cheese, butter, and vanilla until smooth.

Unroll the cake once it is cooled and spread filling evenly over it and then roll it back up.

Serve immediately or refrigerate for up to a few days. These can also be frozen.

32. Raspberry Ricotta Cake

Inspired by *Bon Appétit*.

This is just an elegant cake made with simple ingredients.

Total time: 1 hour, 15 minutes
Serves: 8

Ingredients

cooking spray
1 1/2 cups flour
1 cup sugar
2 teaspoons baking powder
1 teaspoon kosher salt
3 large eggs
1 1/2 cups ricotta cheese
1 teaspoon vanilla
1 stick unsalted butter, melted
1 cup frozen raspberries or blackberries, divided

Directions

Preheat oven to 350 F.

Line a round 9-inch cake pan with parchment paper and lightly coat with cooking spray.

Whisk flour, sugar, baking powder, and salt in a large bowl.

Whisk eggs, ricotta, and vanilla in a medium bowl until smooth.

Fold wet ingredients into dry ingredients until just blended.

Next, fold in butter, followed by 3/4 cup raspberries, taking care not to crush berries.

Scrape batter into prepared pan and scatter remaining raspberries over the top.

Bake cake until golden brown and a tester inserted into center comes out clean, 50–55 minutes. Let cool at least 20 minutes.

This cake can be made two days ahead. Store tightly wrapped at room temperature.

33. Rhubarb Dessert

Inspired by Janet Finn, our neighbor from Dalton, Pennsylvania.

Rhubarb is not always easy to find these days, even though it grows like a weed. It is worth looking for in June because it makes a lovely dessert.

Total time: 55 minutes
Serves: 12

Ingredients

5 cups fresh rhubarb cut into chunks or 2 (16-ounce) bags frozen cut rhubarb
1 cup sugar
1 (3-ounce) package strawberry gelatin
1/2 package white cake mix
1 cup water
1/2 cup butter

Directions

Heat oven to 350 degrees F.

Put rhubarb in an oblong 2-quart baking dish. Sprinkle with sugar and dry gelatin. Toss and mix, spreading the fruit evenly in the dish.

In a medium-sized bowl, mix the remaining ingredients with wooden spoon until well blended and then pour over rhubarb.

Bake 40–45 minutes until golden brown on top.

Let stand 10 minutes.

Serve warm with ice cream.

I use a bigger dish, use a bit more rhubarb, and double the batter.

34. Strawberry Shortcake

Inspired by the back of the Bisquick box from forty-five years ago.

Total time 25 min
Makes 8–10 cakes

Ingredients

2 cups Bisquick
3 tablespoons shortening, melted
5 tablespoons sugar, divided
2/3 cup milk
sliced strawberries
whipped cream for topping

Directions

Heat oven to 450 degrees F.

Whisk together Bisquick, shortening, 3 tablespoons sugar, and milk until smooth batter forms.

Place heaping tablespoon of batter on baking sheet sprayed with cooking spray.

Bake until golden, 10–12 minutes.

Cool shortcakes completely.

Mix remaining sugar with strawberries and let sit at room temperature for at least an hour.

Serve shortcakes topped with sliced strawberries and whipped cream

35. Tandy Cakes

Inspired by Aunt Janine.

Total time: 40 minutes plus chill time
Serves: 12

Ingredients

Sponge Cake Layer
4 eggs
2 cups sugar
2 cups flour

1 cup scalded milk
2 tablespoons butter

Peanut Butter Layer
1 (12- or 18-ounce) jar peanut butter

Chocolate Frosting Layer
1/2 cup butter
1/2 cup cocoa

1 (16-ounce) box powdered sugar
1/3 cup milk

Directions

Preheat oven to 350 degrees F.

Spray a jelly roll pan with cooking spray.

Beat sugar and eggs together.

Add flour and mix well.

Melt butter in scalded milk and add to mixture. Pour batter into greased jelly roll pan.

Bake 20 minutes or until cake is just browning on the edges and no longer dents with touched.

Spread peanut butter onto hot cake. Cool just slightly and then refrigerate until chilled.

Melt butter over low to medium heat. Add cocoa and bring to a boil.

Remove from heat and add powdered sugar and milk.

Mix well. Carefully spread frosting over chilled peanut butter layer.

Refrigerate until chocolate is set.

Serve at room temperature or cold.

Keep refrigerated.

36. Tres Leches Cake

Inspired by Food Network.

Made with three milks, I make this cake every May to celebrate Cinco de Mayo.

Prep time: 25 minutes
Total time: 1 hour, 20 minutes
Serves: 10–12

Ingredients

1 1/2 cups flour
2 teaspoons baking powder
1 teaspoon kosher salt
3 extra-large eggs at room temperature
1 cup plus 5 tablespoons sugar, divided
2 teaspoons vanilla
1/2 cup milk
1 1/4 cups heavy cream
1 (12-ounce) can evaporated milk
1 (14- ounces) can sweetened condensed milk
1/2 teaspoon almond extract
seeds scraped from 1 vanilla bean (If I do not have these on hand, I use 1 teaspoon vanilla.)
8 cups fresh strawberries for serving
sifted powdered sugar for dusting
whipped cream for topping

Directions

Preheat oven to 350 degrees F.

Butter a 9- x 13-inch baking pan.

Sift flour, baking powder, and salt into a small bowl and set aside.

Place the eggs, 1 cup sugar, and vanilla in the bowl of an electric mixer fitted with paddle attachment. Beat on medium-high speed for 10 minutes until light and fluffy. (I know this is a long time, but do it.)

Reduce speed to low and slowly add half the flour mixture, then the milk, and finally the remaining flour mixture.

Mix with a rubber spatula to be sure the batter is mixed well.

Pour batter in to prepared pan, smooth the top, and bake for 25 minutes, until the cake springs back when touched lightly in the middle and a cake tester comes out clean.

Set aside and cool for 30 minutes.

In a 4-cup liquid measuring cup, whisk together the heavy cream, evaporated milk, sweetened condensed milk, almond extract, and vanilla seed.

Using a bamboo skewer, poke holes all over the cooked cake and slowly pour the cream mixture over the cake, allowing it to be absorbed completely before continuing to pour on more of the mixture.

Cover the cake with plastic wrap and refrigerate for at least 6 hours.

To serve, toss the strawberries with 5 tablespoons sugar. Dust cake with powdered sugar. Serve with a dollop of whipped cream.

37. Zucchini Chocolate Cake

Inspired by my Mom.

At the end of summer when you don't know what to do with all the zucchini, try this. It is moist, very chocolaty, and takes little time to make.

Total time: 1 hour
Serves: 10–12

Ingredients

2 cups flour
1 teaspoon baking powder
1 teaspoon baking soda
1 1/2 teaspoons nutmeg
1 1/2 teaspoons cinnamon
1 1/2 teaspoons salt
1/4 cup cocoa
3 eggs
2 cups sugar
1/2 cup oil
3/4 cup buttermilk (I have also used heavy cream.)
2 cups shredded zucchini
3/4 cup chopped walnuts
1 teaspoon vanilla
1 teaspoon orange peel
1/2–3/4 cups chocolate chips (optional)

Directions

Preheat oven to 350 degrees F.

Sift dry ingredients together.

Beat eggs, sugar, and oil.

Stir in flour with buttermilk and zucchini.

Blend well. Add walnuts, vanilla, and orange peel. Mix in chocolate chips if using.

Bake in a tube pan for 45 minutes.

38. Biscotti (Anicini)

Inspired by Il Fornaio.

This is a *great* biscotti recipe. There are many versions of this classic Italian cookie, but this tops them all. To me, a good biscotti should not crack your teeth when you bite into it. The outside should have a reasonable crunch, and the inside should be delightfully soft and full of taste. This is perfect with just about anything—a cup of coffee, a cup of tea, a glass of wine, or just by itself.

Total time: 45 minutes
Makes about 30–35 cookies

Ingredients

2 1/3 cups unbleached flour
1 teaspoon baking powder
1/2 teaspoon salt
1 tablespoon aniseeds
1 1/2 cups sliced raw almonds
1 stick unsalted butter at room temperature
1 1/4 cups sugar
3 eggs
1/2 teaspoon vanilla
1/4 teaspoon anise extract
additional flour for work surface
1/2–3/4 cup dried cranberries

Directions

Preheat oven to 375 degrees F.

In a bowl, stir together the flour, baking powder, salt, aniseeds, and almonds. Set aside.

In a large mixing bowl, combine the butter and sugar. Using handheld mixer set on medium speed, beat the ingredients until the mixture is fluffy, light, and pale in color, about 5 minutes.

Continuing to bet on medium speed, adding eggs, one at a time, beating well after each addition.

Beat in the vanilla and anise extracts.

Reduce the speed to low and add the flour mixture, one third at a time, beating well after each addition until thoroughly incorporated. Beat until a smooth dough forms.

Add cranberries and mix thoroughly.

Turn the dough out onto a lightly floured work surface and divide into four equal portions.

Using the palms of your hands, roll each portion into a log about 12 inches long and 1 1/2 inches in diameter.

Line a 12-inch wide baking sheet that is at least 18 inches long with parchment paper or grease it with butter.

Place the logs crosswise on the baking sheet, spacing them 3 inches apart.

Using the palm of your hand, lightly flatten the top of each log until it is 1/2 inch thick.

Bake the logs in the preheated oven until a light golden brown, about 18 minutes.

Remove from the oven and let cool on the baking sheets until they can be handled, about 10 minutes. Leave the oven on at 375 degrees.

Transfer the logs to a cutting surface. With a sharp knife, cut them crosswise on the diagonal into slices 1/2 inch wide.

Arrange the pieces cut side down onto the baking sheet lined with parchment.

Return the cookies to the oven and bake until toasted and the edges are golden, 8–10 minutes.

Let cool completely on baking sheets. Store in a covered container at room temperature for up to 2 weeks.

39. Flourless Chocolate Torte

Inspired by my childhood friend, Margi.

Margi and I have been friends since we were twelve years old. To say she has been a faithful friend is an understatement. On top of that, she can really cook!

This is a chocolate lover's dream!

Total time: 50 minutes plus chilling time
Serves: 8

Ingredients

Cake
unsweetened cocoa powder for dusting
10 ounces bittersweet chocolate, finely chopped
1/4 cup unsalted butter, cut into 6 pieces, plus extra for greasing
5 large egg yolks
1/4 cup plus 2 tablespoons sugar, divided
1 tablespoon dark rum or brewed espresso (optional)
1 teaspoon vanilla
pinch salt
3 large egg whites at room temperature

Glaze
1/2 cup butter cut into 4 pieces
8 ounces bittersweet chocolate, chopped
2 tablespoons light corn syrup

Directions

For the Cake
Preheat the oven to 300 degrees F.

Grease the bottom of a round 8-inch cake pan and line it with parchment paper. Grease the paper and the side of the pan and then dust with cocoa powder.

On the top of a double boiler, combine the chocolate and 3/4 cup butter. Set over barely simmering water and melt, whisking until blended. Set aside to cool slightly.

In a large bowl, with the mixer set on medium-high speed, beat together the egg yolks, 1/4 cup sugar, rum, vanilla, and salt until pale and very thick.

Gradually pour into the chocolate mixture and continue beating until well blended.

In a deep, clean bowl, using a mixer on medium-high speed, beat the egg whites until foamy.

Gradually add the remaining sugar and continue to beat until medium-firm peaks form.

Scoop half of the egg whites into the chocolate and fold them in gently.

Fold in the remaining whites until no streaks remain.

Pour the batter into prepared pan and spread it out evenly.

Bake the torte until it puffs slightly and a toothpick inserted into the center comes out very moist but not liquid, about 35 minutes. *Do not* overcook.

Let cool on a rack for 30 minutes.

Run a small knife around the inside of the pan to loosen the cake and then invert onto a flat plate.

Lift off the pan and carefully peel away the parchment paper. Let cool completely.

Cover and refrigerate until very cold, at least 8 hours or overnight.

For the Glaze

Combine 1/2 cup butter and 8 ounces chopped bittersweet chocolate in the top of a double boiler.

Set over barely simmering water and melt, whisking until blended.

Remove from the heat and whisk in 2 tablespoons light corn syrup until smooth and glossy.

Set the cake on a wire rack over a large plate or baking sheet.

Slowly pour the warm glaze over the center of the cake. The glaze should cover the surface evenly spilling over the edges and running down the sides. The excess will fall on the plate below.

Refrigerate cake until firm, at least 2 hours.

Transfer to a flat serving plate.

Using a thin-bladed knife, cut the cake into slices, dipping the knife into hot water and wiping it dry before each cut.

Garnish with raspberries or strawberries

40. Chocolate Eclair Cake

Inspired by my friend, Mary Beth Weber.

Mary Beth's son Robert met Cody in first grade, and they were friends until he died. One of my son's greatest gifts to me as a mother was the gift of meeting so many nice parents. Mary Beth and her husband, Rob, have been part of our lives for a very long time, and they continue to be devoted friends

Total time: 30 minutes
Serves: 8-10

Ingredients

2 packages vanilla instant pudding mix
3 cups milk
12 ounces frozen whipped topping
2 packages graham crackers

Directions

Blend milk and vanilla pudding for about 2 minutes.

Fold in whipped topping.

Layer graham crackers on bottom of dish.

Pour half the pudding mixture over the crackers.

Then layer more crackers and pour the second half of pudding mix over them.

End with another layer of crackers.

Top with frosting. (Recipe to follow.)

Frosting
3 tablespoons milk
3 tablespoons butter
3 tablespoons cocoa
1 cup powdered sugar

Heat butter and milk to combine.

Add cocoa and powdered sugar and mix well.

Spread over cake.

41. The Best Carrot Cake

Inspired by *Bon Appétit*.

Total time: 1 1/2 hours plus chilling time
Serves: 12

This cake is a winner! It truly is one of the best carrot cakes ever, and we can't do Easter without it.

Ingredients

Cake
cooking spray
3/4 cup golden raisins (optional)
3 tablespoons dark rum (optional)
1 cup chopped walnuts
1 pound carrots, coarsely grated
1 cup buttermilk at room temperature
2 1/2 cups flour
2 teaspoons cinnamon
2 teaspoons ginger
1/2 teaspoon nutmeg
2 teaspoons baking powder
1 1/2 teaspoons kosher salt
3/4 teaspoon baking soda
4 large eggs at room temperature
1 cup granulated sugar
3/4 cup packed dark brown sugar
2 teaspoons vanilla extract
3/4 cup vegetable oil

Frosting
1 1/2 (8-ounce) packages cream cheese at room temperature
3/4 cup (1 1/2 sticks) unsalted butter at room temperature
1 teaspoon vanilla
generous pinch kosher salt
4 cups powdered sugar

Directions

Preheat oven to 350 degrees F.

Lightly coat two round 9-inch diameter cake pans with cooking spray and line bottoms with parchment paper. Lightly coat parchment with cooking spray also.

Heat raisins and rum in a small pan over low heat just until warm, about 2 minutes. Remove from heat and let sit until liquid is absorbed and raisins are plump, 15–20 minutes.

Meanwhile, toast walnuts on a rimmed baking sheet, tossing once, until golden brown, 8–10 minutes. Let cool.

Combine carrots and buttermilk in a medium bowl.

Whisk flour, cinnamon, ginger, nutmeg, baking powder, salt, and baking soda in a large bowl.

Using an electric mixer on high speed, beat eggs, both sugars, and vanilla until pale and thick, about 4 minutes.

Reduce speed to medium-low and gradually stream in oil.

Add dry ingredients in three additions, alternating with carrot mixture in two additions, beginning and ending with dry ingredients. Mix until smooth.

Fold in raisins and walnuts.

Scrape batter into prepared pans.

Bale cakes, rotating pans halfway through, until a tester inserted into the middle comes out clean, 35–45 minutes.

Transfer pans to a wire rack and let cool 10 minutes.

Run a knife around sides of cakes and invert onto wire rack. Remove parchment and let cool completely.

Using an electric mixer on high speed, beat cream cheese and butter in a medium bowl until smooth, about 1 minute.

Beat in vanilla extract and salt.

Reduce speed to low and gradually mix in powdered sugar.

Increase speed to high and beat frosting until light and fluffy, about 2 minutes.

Place one cake, dome side down, on a platter. Spread 3/4 cup frosting evenly over the top.

Place remaining cake, dome side down, on top.

Spread top and sides with 1 1/4 cups frosting and chill 30 minutes to let frosting set.

Spread remaining frosting over top and sides, swirling decoratively.

42. Dutch Oven Peach Cobbler

Inspired by MyRecipes.

This recipe is meant to be made over a fire. I have made it in my oven—certainly not as adventurous but equally as delicious.

Total time: 30 minutes
Serves: 6

Ingredients

2 pounds frozen peaches
1 teaspoon cinnamon
3/4 cup sugar, divided
1 cup pancake mix
1/4 cup butter, cut into 1/8-inch pieces
1 large egg
sweetened whipped cream

I double the topping because I like a bit more batter than this makes.

Directions

Heat oven to 350 degrees F.

Mix peaches, cinnamon, and 1/2 cup sugar in a 4- to 6-quart cast iron pan or Dutch oven.

Stir pancake mix, butter, egg, remaining 1/4 cup sugar, and 1/4 cup water in a medium bowl to make a thick and chunky batter.

Drop four evenly spaced heaping spoonfuls of batter over peaches. If you double the batter, you will have more spoonfuls to drop.

Bake for 25 minutes until batter is puffed and starting to brown.

Serve with whipped cream

43. The Best Sugar Cookie Ever

Inspired by Sheila, my loyal and faithful friend

Total time: 1 hour, 20 minutes
Makes about 40 cutout cookies

Ingredients

2 cups flour
1/2 teaspoon salt
1/4 teaspoon baking powder
3/4 cup butter
2/3 cup granulated sugar
1 large egg
1 1/2 teaspoons vanilla

Directions

Combine flour, salt, and baking powder and set aside.

Combine butter and sugar and beat until fluffy.

Add the egg and beat.

Add vanilla and beat.

Reduce mixer speed to medium and add dry ingredients.

Form into a ball.

Chill for 1 hour.

Roll out the dough and cut into desired shapes.

Bake on parchment-lined baking sheet for 9 minutes or until edges are lightly browned.

44. Sheila's Banana Cake

Inspired by Sheila.

Banana cake is one of those desserts that is a staple on the dessert menu. This one is luscious.

Total time: 1 hour
Serves: 12–16

Ingredients

Cake
3 eggs
2 bananas (overripe are best)
1 cup (2 sticks) unsalted butter
2 cups sugar
3 cups flour
1 1/2 teaspoons baking powder
1 1/2 teaspoons baking soda
1 teaspoon vanilla
1 1/4 cup buttermilk

Icing
1 cup (2 sticks) unsalted butter
1 cup sugar
1 teaspoon vanilla
3/4 cup warm milk

Directions

For the Cake
Preheat oven to 350 degrees F.

Grease two 8- x 8-inch pans.

Cream butter and sugar until fluffy.

Add bananas (break into small pieces for easier mixing).

Add remaining ingredients and mix well.

Divide mixture between pans.

Bake for 40–45 minutes. Cakes are done when a knife inserted in center of cake comes out clean.

For the Icing
Cream butter and sugar.

Add vanilla and mix.

Add the warm milk in a steady stream with mixer running.

Beat until it's the consistency of whipped cream

Ice cakes when completely cool

45. Peanut Tunnel of Fudge Cake

Inspired by Food Network.

Total time: 4 hours, 45 minutes (cooling time: 4 hours)
Serves: 8–10

This is one great cake! It has everything: chocolate, peanuts, *and* peanut butter! And the middle is gooey!

Ingredients

Cake
cooking spray
2 1/4 cups flour
2 cups honey-roasted peanuts
2 tablespoons peanut butter powder (optional, but I recommend it)
4 large eggs plus 2 egg yolks
1 1/2 cups (2 1/2 sticks) unsalted butter, cut into pieces at room temperature
1 1/2 cups granulated sugar
3/4 cup packed dark brown sugar
1/3 cup roasted peanut oil
2 teaspoons pure vanilla extract
1/2 teaspoon kosher salt
1 1/2 cups powdered sugar
3/4 cup unsweetened cocoa powder

Glaze
1 1/2 cups powdered sugar
3 tablespoons milk
1/4 cup creamy peanut butter
1 teaspoon vanilla extract
1/4 teaspoon kosher salt

Directions

For the Cake
Position a rack in the lower third of the oven and preheat to 350 degrees F.

Generously coat a 10- to 15-cup Bundt pan with cooking spray.

Combine the flour, peanuts, and peanut butter powder in a large bowl.

Lightly stir the eggs and egg yolks in a bowl with a fork until they are just streaky. Set aside.

Beat the butter in a large bowl with a mixer on medium speed until fluffy, about 2 minutes.

Add the granulated sugar and brown sugar to the butter and beat until fluffy, about 4 minutes.

Beat in the peanut oil, vanilla, and salt. Scrape down the sides of the bowl.

Reduce the mixer speed to low and add beaten eggs in three additions.

Beat in the powdered sugar and cocoa powder until just combined. *Do not* overmix.

Fold in the flour and peanut mixture with a rubber spatula.

Pour the batter into the prepared Bundt pan and spread it evenly. Bake 45 minutes, being careful not to overbake.

Transfer to a rack and let cool 20 minutes in the pan. Gently press down the cake to remove any air bubbles in the tunnel. It is OK if the cake cracks a little bit. Cool for 3 hours.

For the Glaze
Whisk in the powdered sugar, milk, peanut butter, vanilla, and salt in a medium bowl until smooth.

Invert the cake onto a plate and pour glaze on top.

Chapter 8:

Then There Was COVID-19

2020 will forever be remembered as an historic time. COVID-19 turned us upside down and inside out. I would be remiss to ignore its impact on our universe. It managed to interfere and even stop many important life events.

But our dinners continued. Many were by takeout, but they continued.

When the rate of transmission was reasonable during the summer and fall months, dinners were outside when the weather cooperated. It was kids only, and adults stayed home. I was not about to let this virus be in charge.

Joseph, along with the other foundation members, were determined to do something to recognize Cody despite COVID-19. A three-on-three tournament and evening with five hundred people were not possible, but doing nothing was not acceptable.

Once again, the kids thought outside the box.

Instead of a three-on-three tournament, they orchestrated a shoot-out where only five contestants would be in the gym at one time, spread very far apart. More than eighty shooters participated. All appropriate precautions were enforced, and the day turned out to be fabulous.

The basket raffle was held outdoors as well as online. Cars filled with people stopped by all day long to try their best at winning. Continue Cody's Commitment was held virtually via a video created by one of the kids.

Our goal was to fulfill our mission to remember Cody, educate students, and promote organ donor awareness. None of us expected to raise much money. Once again, our devoted sponsors reached deep into their souls as well as their pockets to support our cause.

In the end, it was another job well done.

Those who played had fun, and Cody's spirit was yet again brought alive.

The kids would not let this plague win.

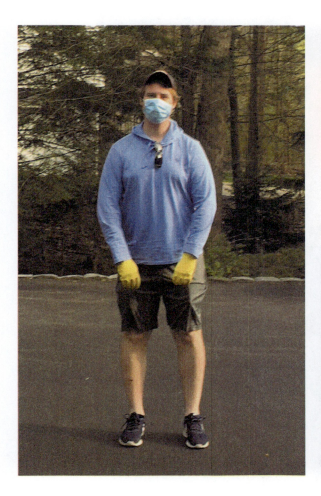
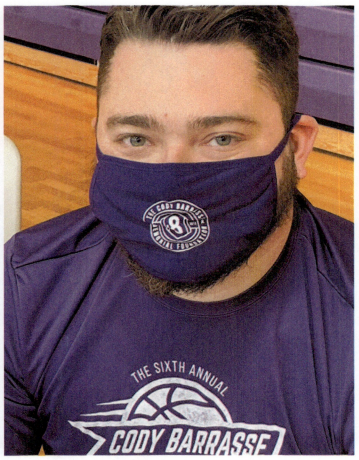

Epilogue

So, now you have seen one hundred months of recipes.

You have read the many stories about my Cody.

You have seen what real friendship means.

And you have witnessed the powerful force of the determined young people who created this incredible foundation.

In the introduction, I wrote that this is a non-cookbook and really a Love story.

Love among young men and women called friends.

Love from my friends who help give me the courage to be the mother I need to be.

Love from a Mother for her precious sons.

I hope you agree.

In life, we can be stripped of so much. There is no guarantee that everything will be OK. You *can* be guaranteed that it will be not OK. Our prayer must be only for acceptance.

But let it be clear: *Nothing* can rob us of Love.

Not any person, not any distance, not any circumstance … can steal Love from us.

Not even Death.

And in our case, the vehicle that we used to allow Love to win was food.

Cody was the quintessential athlete. He could do it all. He was particularly passionate about football. His jersey number while at Scranton Prep was 8. Our logo has the number 8 at its centerpiece. This is the eighth year since his death. The one hundredth dinner falls on the weekend of Cody's tournament and evening celebration. It happens to be in the eighth month. There are no coincidences in this thing we call Life.

From the time my children were born, I would say, "I love you to infinity." The number 8 on its side happens to be the infinity sign.

So, as I close, I will say, as I always do to my children:

I love you …

To infinity. → ∞

Linda

About the Author

For this first-time author, who was raised in an Italian American home, food was always a focal point. As Linda raised her own children, food yet again played an important part in day-to-day life. Dinner was the time when her family connected. It was not just about the eating. It was about the preparation, the smells, the discussions, and, most importantly, the love.

Linda, along with her friends, have been cooking for one hundred dinners. These, however, are no ordinary dinners. They are dinners to soothe their souls after losing her son Cody in April 2013. Her friends are just as integral to this book as she is.

Her hope is that along with experiencing fun and excellent recipes, her readers will understand how tragedy will *never* trump love. In this case, food was love's catalyst that resulted in The Cody Barrasse Memorial Foundation.

This group has decided to make something beautiful out of something tragic. Hopefully, their lives are filled with more meaning. Hopefully, the sting of their loss hurts a bit less. And hopefully, their bellies and souls have been filled with comforting food and love.